Chicks:
A User's Guide to Dating,
Love and Sex

Chicks:
A User's Guide to Dating,
Love and Sex

By

Dag Albright

New Tradition Books

Chicks: A User's Guide to Dating, Love and Sex
by
Dag Albright

New Tradition Books
ISBN 1932420592

For the Guys who are after the Chicks

Contents

The confusing world of chicks.

There are a lot of guys out there who have one thing in common: They all want to know what's up with chicks. They just don't "get" chicks, they just don't understand them and, thusly, they just don't know how to approach, let alone date them. They also get extremely nervous whenever they're around women. Well, join the club. Most guys get nervous when they're around a new girl for the first time.

There's nothing wrong with guys like this. They just don't know "what to do" or "what to say". And they don't "do" anything and rarely "say" anything. Chicks become islands to which they'll never swim or experience. To them, chicks remain a mystery, one that can't really be solved with common sense or a formula. When this happens, a guy can be left feeling a little isolated and lonely. Sometimes, this leads to resentment and hostility. Even worse, sometimes it can lead to them totally withdrawing from the dating scene.

It doesn't have to be like this.

I know that chicks can be confusing. I know that they can be a mystery. You say or do one "wrong" thing and they write you off. Or, they're so intimidating at first that it's hard to just walk up to them and say "Hi". Chicks can also seem off-putting and a little stuck-up, but the reality is, most women are just like most men in some respects. They, too, are a bit confused about dating and love and sex.

What this means is that everybody is pretty much in the same boat. When this happens, no one wants to make that first move because we're all afraid of rejection. We don't want to be laughed at. And no one wants to feel like their efforts are being wasted. As a result of this, a lot of people remain alone.

This seems to happen a lot in the dating world. The problem is that none of us have ever really been sat down and taught how to interact with the opposite sex. From an early age, we just stared longingly across the playground at the girls and wondered what to do. The girls stared at us, we stared at them, and neither of us made a move. And it doesn't get much better when we're adults. Who hasn't been out at a club staring over towards a group of the opposite sex with the same uncertainty we felt as kids? Only this time, there's more pressure to perform. We know the ladies are waiting on us to make a move and are resenting the fact that we're not. And, usually, we let that opportunity pass us by, all because we're too scared to make that first move.

I know some guys hold back more than others. They just can't get the nerve up to approach a girl. As a result, they go nowhere and wonder why they always go to the movies alone. It's not their fault, per se. They just don't know what to do. Not many of us are born with that natural-born instinct that tells us how to make a girl interested in us, or even allows us to recognize when she is interested in us. We're not that lucky, as they say. However, there is something you can do about this.

You, too, can attract females. The great thing is, it doesn't take much. What it mostly takes is a little initiative and some nerve. Along with this, a little bit of confidence and you'll be on your way. But how do you get this confidence? How do you know how to deal with chicks? It will come but it takes some know-how and practice. Sure, in hindsight, it would have been nice to have an older brother or a cool dad that had all the answers to chicks and their mysteries. But the reality is, our older brothers and fathers usually know less than we do. Perhaps our fathers just got lucky when they met our mothers.

And maybe you haven't been quite so lucky. Maybe, for you, it's not about how to get back into the game but how to get the game started. This is what this book is going to teach you. It's all about the confusing world of chicks and how to figure them out.

Not to over-generalize, but most men do not have a clue about how to romance girls. They don't know anything about flowers or dinners or etiquette. All they know is that women usually intimidate them. They're afraid of rejection and of being laughed at. Well, get over it. We're all afraid of that. But the man who tries is the man who gets the girl. Standing by and holding the wall up is only an option for the weak at heart. When dealing with women, as per my experiences, a guy can't just blend into the background. You have to stand out. In a nutshell, *you have to let her know you're alive.*

This is not to say that you have to be loud and obnoxious to draw the attention to yourself. You don't have to make a fool out of yourself. You don't need a "game play" and you don't need a hundred-thousand dollar sports car. All you need is what you were born with and that all boils down to confidence.

In essence: If you're willing to put yourself out there, you can do this, you can get a girl to talk to you and, perhaps, go out with you. It might take some work, but it's not beyond your reach. It's all up to you to put this into motion. Once you understand that and vow to do it, then you can move forward and into the dating scene.

Becoming a pro at dating takes time, effort and work. And it will be work, so be warned. However, if you can commit yourself to this, your whole world will open up. You'll actually have something to do on the weekends, something to look forward to! And, believe me, I know how important this can be to a lonely guy. Many guys don't think they'll ever be able to land a girl. This isn't true. All it takes is the first step in the right direction and I hope this book can do that for you.

Having said all that, let's get to it because there is some work to be done before you make that first move. But you have to be willing to take on the task. If not, then this will be ready for you when you are. It's all about preparation and honesty, as you will find out in the following chapters.

I'm just a normal person. These are just my observations and what I've done to improve myself and my chances at dating. I've helped and observed many a man and learned not only from my mistakes, but from the mistakes of others. Women are a mystery but not a mystery that can't be solved. It just takes some know-how and some diligence to become the guy that women not only like, but want to date. Let's face it, being stuck in the "friend" zone sucks. But being someone who is seen as a potential romantic interest opens up all kinds of opportunities, even if you're not ready to settle down just yet.

Dating is fun. Looking for a potential life-partner should be seen a challenge, but shouldn't overwhelm you. This is stuff people have been doing since the beginning of time. It's not that hard. What's hard is the fact that over the last few years, dating has gotten this sort of score-card mentality. We think we have to check off a list of things we want in a potential mate. And all we really need is the ability to be compatible with someone and the confidence to follow through. After that, the rest should come easy.

What's it's all about in the end.

Before we begin, let me say something about love. It's just my opinion but I think love is one of the most misunderstood things in the world. Love is an emotion, but it can really become confusing to try and explain it. Also, love isn't just a means to an end; it's about connecting with someone on an emotional level.

Why is all this important to say right off? Because love is what we all want, deep down inside. Not to sound corny, but it's true. Sure, we want to shop around at first and we want to have fun, but the ultimate goal of dating is to find love and to settle down, right? This may not happen for years, but it's really what most of us aspire to. We want love in the end. Why? Because connecting like that to another human being is real and most of us are starved for something real, something we can totally relate to. Having something real in our lives makes it all worthwhile. Sure, it's great to date the hot chick with the hot bod. But if we never connect to her and she never connects to us, we end up feeling empty.

So, what is love? To me, love isn't about finding a soul mate. Love is about two people who meet and, at that moment, are both ready to open up to the possibility of love.

It's about the desire to be with someone rather than just having desire *for* someone.

This is what dating is ultimately all about. And becoming the best you can be is where it starts. For, if she sees you at your best, she will be open to what you have to offer. And that's all there really is to it. In the end, all you have to do is take that first step to becoming a better man and to getting what matters most in the end, love.

Your expectations.

The most important thing to realize is that dating is less about the woman you're dating than about you and your expectations. Women aren't that hard to figure out. What's hard to figure out is what *you* want and what *you* expect from a woman. If you know, for instance, that a woman is highly unlikely to put out on the first date, your expectations of this will be very low. However, if you also know that most women want to settle down and have kids "some day", then you can go in with a more open-mind and see if you'd like to pursue this with her. If this makes you want to run, you can run, certainly, or you can stick around and see what happens.

You have to understand that most women know what they're after when they go out with a guy. They know whether it's just for fun or if they're looking for a boyfriend or a husband. And, while they might not be looking for a boyfriend, they're always open to the possibilities. Once you do the same thing, you can really being to visualize your future and what you want, which will help you narrow down what sort of chick you want to spend your time with.

Finding out about who you are and what you want is just as important as learning the ropes about dating in general. Figuring out your expectations of each date is important, too. If you expect too much going in, then you're surely to be disappointed. But if you don't expect each date to be a life-changing experience, the date becomes about having a good time and not just about finding a life-partner. This allows you to relax and once you relax, then your date can relax and you can do what you're there for: To get to know one another better to see if you want to pursue a future date or relationship with this person.

In the end, you're the one who will have to live with his choices. Making the right choices is what it's all about. It's not just about finding one perfect girl. It's about finding the one perfect girl *for you*. In the meanwhile, you can just have fun trying to find her.

What the hell happened to me?

Let's do a scenario, okay? Let's take a look at a guy I know. His name's Joe. He was just an average guy in his mid-twenties who'd been through a few bad breakups and had started to find himself spending more and more time alone. He used to go out and meet women. He used to not take himself too seriously. But that didn't matter now. Something had changed him, though he couldn't exactly put his finger on what it was.

Even though he wanted more out of life, it just became too much of a hassle to put himself out there. He became content to sit at home with the TV and forget about everything else that was out there in the world. Chicks didn't seem to dig him and whenever the thought about going out arose, he'd ask himself the invariable self-pitying question of, *Why bother? Aren't they just going to reject me anyway?*

With an attitude like that, is it any wonder Joe didn't go out? He'd given up on life. He'd lost his confidence through a few bad experiences and had let his body go to pot. *Why work out and eat right when no one notices?* In essence, Joe had stopped caring about himself.

I know Joe. You know Joe, too. He is me and he is you. He is all of us. We all have this capacity to take a bad experience and make it into a life-stunting event. We stop living life due to our fear of being further rejected and/or humiliated. We just stop living and hoping for a brighter future. It's hard to swallow, but for some, this is a reality.

However, one day, Joe woke up. He was standing in front of a mirror in a department store and noticed a very out of shape guy staring back at him. At first, he didn't recognize this guy and wondered how anyone could look so bad. But then, to his astonishment, he realized he *was* that guy in the mirror. He didn't only look unhealthy, he looked gray, like he was barely even there.

Joe felt something then, something akin to panic. He was only in his twenties and this was how he had ended up? He ran out of the store and home where he further observed himself in the mirror. He hadn't shaved in days. But that didn't matter, he had a dead-end job and his boss didn't care how he looked. Once again he was struck with the thought, "Why should I care if no one else does?"

But then something struck Joe. How was anyone going to ever care about him if he didn't care about himself? And who was going to care when all he could do was stand around and pity himself to death?

He wasn't a bad guy, just a guy who'd been rejected some and felt like crap about himself. He'd lost his self-confidence and his ability to feel hopeful. He wondered how he had let this happen and then it just occurred to him: He'd let the opinion of others—or rather how he perceived how others thought of him—get in the way of his life and of his happiness. He vowed that day to change for the better and to kick-start his life. Nothing was worth the misery he was putting himself through.

It doesn't matter what happened to Joe after that because Joe is fictitious, but you aren't. If you've ever felt this way, ask yourself now: What the hell happened to me? Do a little soul-searching. Write about it in a journal or see a therapist if you think it will help. The point is to get all this crap out of your mind so you can get out there and into the dating game.

This is the first step in getting your life on track if you've found yourself in this predicament. If this doesn't apply to you, then move on to the next chapter. If it does, sit down and figure it out and then move on. There are brighter days ahead.

It's important not to bring a lot baggage into any new relationship and feeling like crap about yourself because of bad past experiences is exactly what baggage is. When you do this, you will start feeling inadequate or hurt and, when and if you get a girlfriend, you will begin to blame her for this. She won't stick around too long if you do this. No one wants to be blamed for something they didn't do. This is what having baggage does, though. It will make you blame an innocent person because you haven't faced your feelings of rejection or inadequacy yet and this will make you strike out and want to hurt them, because you can't face the hurt that's been done to you. You will want to make someone pay for what happened to you. But you can't do that or you'll never have a relationship. What you have to keep in mind is that these feelings of rejection and inadequacy are just that—feelings! Just because someone made you feel inadequate doesn't mean you are! In the end, all baggage does is weigh a new relationship down and eventually smother it to death.

You might be asking—"What does this have to do with dating?" Everything! Taking responsibility for yourself means getting rid of any baggage you might have the best way you can. Not all guys have baggage, but most of us do, to some extent. And baggage can do us damage, whether it makes us want to crawl into a hole and hide for the rest of our lives or become abusive and controlling in our relationships. What we do with our baggage will set the pattern for what our dating lives will become. Learning to leave it alone is the best thing you can do with it. Getting over feeling of "not being good enough" is a step in the right direction. Once you stop believing you're a bad person, you can start being a good person, one who can quite possibly make a woman or two pretty damn happy.

While this may seem dreary and out of place for a dating book, this has happened to a lot of people I know. The point is to recognize it now and move forward. Without first looking into the mirror, there can be no self-improvement. And, also, if you think you're not worth it, no girl is going to think you're worth it, either. It is first up to us to set ourselves straight. This isn't anyone's job but our own and to expect someone to come into our lives and "make it right", which is about like waiting for your fairy godmother to materialize and give you a million dollars. Most women are looking for someone with confidence and a good attitude. They don't want the depressed dude who never leaves the house unless it's absolutely necessary. After all, how fun would this guy be to hang out with?

The thing is, all you have to do is recognize what's happened to you and make peace with it. Sure, it can still sting a little, but to allow things like this to control you is to also allow yourself to stay stuck. *And no one makes you stay stuck but yourself.* No one stops you unless you allow it.

So, get moving. There is a whole new world out there waiting for you. All you have to do is get ready for it. And all you have to do is take that first step. And it starts with putting down your baggage and moving in a better direction.

We've all been hurt.

As covered in the previous chapter, let me reiterate by saying it again and in a different way: We've all been hurt. We've all been humiliated and we've all been rejected at one time or another. Even good looking guys, even millionaires, even guys who drive expensive sports cars. It happens to everyone at one time or another. We can either make it into a life-changing event, or we can learn and grow and thusly, move on from it.

Think about your life-changing event. Write about it, talk about it to a trusted friend or relative or even a therapist. There is nothing wrong with the way you feel. What's wrong is keeping it bottled up and letting it fester inside of you. Feel the pain you've been avoiding and then move on. It's really that easy. *Don't ever let it stop you from improving yourself.* The thing is, you will either do it or not. It's your choice. Make that choice wisely.

Self-improvement.

One thing I want to really specify in this book is that before you can begin to "get" chicks and all their behaviors, you really need to take a look at yourself first. Before you can know them, you have to know yourself. Remember, it is about you before it is about them. And once you can get your issues taken care of, you'll be better prepared to deal with chicks on the whole.

First and foremost is the assumption many guys have that they are perfect the way they are and could use absolutely no self-improvement. This isn't necessarily true and most every guy can tweak themselves to make themselves better. If you think that you are perfect the way you are, then congratulations. You are in the minority. All of us could use a little improving from time to time.

If we try to improve ourselves and get over the idea that none of us are perfect, we'll be ahead of the game. This starts by accepting the fact that, yeah, you could stand a little self-improvement. If you take the time to do this, you will have a better chance with most chicks out there. If chicks think you take care of yourself, then they think you might be equipped to take care of them, too. This will make them more open and receptive to your advances. It also shows them that you, as a guy, are not a slob and care about how you present yourself.

The best thing to do is ascertain what you need to work on. You can do this by taking a cold, hard look at yourself in the mirror. It's hard, I know, as most of us have had to get in shape at some point in our lives. But just suck it up and do it. Could your body stand to lose a little weight—or a lot? Could you maybe work out and get your muscles in shape? If so, just do it. Working out isn't that hard and losing weight is simple. All you have to do is cut your calories and watch what you eat. Once you get into the habit of doing this, it becomes second-nature and you will automatically begin to do it without thinking. As for working out, you can do the simple calisthenics we all did in gym class—push-ups, sit-ups, etc.—and get a good workout. You don't have to go to a gym, unless, of course, you'd rather.

Next, take a good, hard look in your closet. What's in there? Is it stylish? Is it not? You have to know that having good clothes is important. This doesn't mean you have to spend a fortune or anything, either. It just means that you might have to do a little shopping. If you don't have a clue as to what to buy, ask a female whose style you admire what she thinks is good to wear or just go to the mall and look in the men's department. The basics of nice, button-down shirt, nice pants and good, leather shoes is all you need. Also, good underwear and socks that match your shoes is a good idea. Never wear anything with holes in it.

Keep in mind that most women don't expect you to look like you've stepped out of a magazine. Just look like you're current with the latest styles and care about your appearance. The next thing to check out is your grooming. Do you shave before you go out? And what about your hair? Could it use a trim? Keep these things in check at all times while you're on the dating scene as women really do notice clean-cut, nice looking guys first.

Another thing is to be somewhat meticulous in your bathing. Clean all parts of your body with soap and water. This may seem a bit rudimentary to some, but nobody appreciates a guy who smells like they haven't showered in weeks. Not good as a come-on to any chick or pleasant to anyone in the vicinity, for that matter.

The last thing to be concerned about is your mouth, i.e. your breath. Before you got out, why not floss and brush your teeth, as well as use mouthwash? Another good thing to do is pop a piece of gum or a peppermint into your mouth before approaching a chick. This makes sure you're extra-fresh and you have to know, bad breath is a total turnoff.

This may all seem like "common sense" but I've known guys who wait three or four days between brushing their teeth. And, no, they don't go out much. However, just being reminded of how important these little things are can get you a big return in the end. Good hygiene is crucial if you want to have meaningful relationships with others. Paying attention to all these little things can enable you to be the best you can be at any given time.

The point is that the better you look, the better you take care of yourself, the more women will be attracted to you. Women really don't dig grungy looking guys, even if they are in a rock band. And they definitely don't dig guys who smell bad. You never want to give her a chance to turn you down, do you? By taking care of these simple things like having a good going-out outfit on hand and always keeping your nails clean and trimmed, you will better enable yourself to move forward with more women. I know us guys can sometimes get lazy in our grooming habits, but to appear clean and well-groomed is a must if you are going after women.

By doing simple things like self-improvement, you put yourself out there as a man who is serious about meeting women. If you look—and smell—approachable, you might get lucky and have a few chicks approach you or even ask you out. It's happened before and it can happen to you. You just have to put the effort out. And by knowing you will be getting results back for your efforts will make it all that much easier to do and to get into the habit of. And, really, it all boils down to getting into the habit of looking your best when you go out.

By looking and feeling your best, you're building your confidence, which is what will enable you to push forward to start to seriously meet and date women. This is one of the most important things to understand—confidence is key. There's nothing more vital than confidence. And, what's great about it is the fact that it's relatively easy to obtain if you are willing to put in a little time and effort.

What is dating?

This isn't just an inane question. I think it's very relevant because I think we all get a little confused about what dating really is. Is it meeting for coffee or having a full-fledged relationship? Is it serious or casual? Does it include a gift on Valentine's Day? Is it just a process to find someone to marry?

I think it's all these things. Dating can be fun, causal, and serious. It can be whatever you make it. There seems to be a lot of different variants to dating. I think the best possible way to understand dating is to define dating *for yourself.* The best possible way to do this is to figure out what *you* think dating is and then adjust for each new chick you meet, as she might have a different idea of it as well.

Here's my definition: *Dating is two people getting together and going out somewhere—dinner, movies, park, etc.—in order to interact with one another in an effort to see if they might be compatible to date further.* This may or may not lead to an engagement, marriage and children. It may lead to sex and it may not. It can be serious or causal, depending on the circumstances. Also, it can be a process, a way to get you into a serious relationship.

Dating can be confusing. But, it can also just be fun. You can date a lot of girls without really looking for "the one". Many guys like to date in order to get out of the house and meet new people. Lots of guys I know date a chick, find they aren't compatible with her, and then are introduced by that chick to her friends, whom they can then date. Dating can open up a lot of new doors to many other people, even if you're not exactly compatible with the person you're dating right now.

It's important to keep an open-mind when you're dating so you can take advantage of the situations you find yourself in. Being nice to your date is the key here because, if you are, they'll probably want to keep seeing you, even if it's on a "friend" basis. Getting to that one relationship which may or may not lead to marriage is what the ultimate goal of dating is. And meeting all sorts of new chicks along the way is part of the fun.

Of course, it goes without saying, but no one wants to be in the "friend" zone. But you need to realize that the friend zone can lead to her introducing you to some of her female friends. It can be a good way to network and meet people. Keep in mind that dating can be an introduction into a whole new world of people and new possibilities. It can open you up to more social interaction. It can lead to bigger and better things in your future.

But mostly, dating should be fun, hands down. It shouldn't be taken as seriously as it is. I think we're all in the mindset that if we date someone, all we want to do is see if they're "marriage material". Why not go into a date with nothing on your mind other than having a good time? And, no, I don't mean *that* kind of good time where the night ends in sex, I mean a good experience. Why not go into a date with the idea that you're just getting out of the house to take a cute girl to dinner? It doesn't have to mean anything. It can just mean you're looking for someone to interact with one on one.

Dating can also be done with other people. Yes, you can "double date" and there's even "group dating" going on now where a group of people get together to interact and have a good time. These dates can be fun for everyone involved and can take some of the edge off of having a one-on-one first date.

If we take the seriousness out of it, then everyone can relax and just have a good time. What happens, though, is that we get desperate to find "that someone special" because that's all we've been told to do since we were young: *You have to grow up and get married some day! Hurry up and do it before you're too old!* Well, sure, that's the goal, isn't it? But getting there shouldn't be seen as such a chore, but rather a fun, enlightening experience.

Dating isn't holy matrimony and it's not full-on commitment. It's just that—dating. It's just about meeting someone and having dinner and maybe drinks. It's about finding commonalties. It's about finding out about the person in front of you—*What's she like? What does she do for a living?* It's about sharing part of yourself and interacting. It's about getting out there and interacting with members of the opposite sex.

So, why not take the pressure off both of you and just go into a date looking to have a nice dinner and some good conversation? Why not just be nice and listen to what she's saying and then tell her a little about yourself as the evening progresses? If you're a good first date, she'll think you'll be an even better second date.

Dating is an experience and not just a process. It's one experience in a lifetime of experiences. It won't make or break you. But it can create some nice memories. Look at it as such and relax. That way, if you relax, she'll be able to, too, and you should both be smiling by the end of the evening and looking forward to next time.

Figuring out what's important to you.

What would you rather do? Would you rather hang out with the guys and watch a game or would you rather hang out where available chicks might be? Think about it before you answer. This is something you need to be honest about.

Without the desire to go out and meet women, there's nothing a dating book or anyone can do for you. I've seen it many times. Guys will whine and complain about how there's no women for them, then they take off to a sports bar and spend their paycheck buying rounds for the guys. And the next week, they wonder why they're so lonely—and broke. However, this is a vicious cycle and if you're stuck in it, you should really do something about it.

So ask yourself if you're rather date women or hang out with your buddies? Either answer is fine and it is very important to answer honestly. You can get out there and try to attract females but without the desire to do so, you're playing a losing hand. Your heart will just not be in it. There has to be passion and interest on your part rather than just a vague sense of meeting someone because you think it's something you must do. You don't *have* to do it. It is your life and you can spend it the way you choose.

The point of all this is to let you know that until you are ready to make that first move and get out there and try to meet women, you won't. Nothing is really going to help you.

As I said, spending all your time hanging out with your buddies is fine if that's the way you want to live your life. Nothing's wrong with doing what you want. I know lots of confirmed bachelors who are perfectly happy. It's not that they don't have the ability to meet the right woman, it's just that they don't have the desire.

I know as you read this, it might seem a little confusing. But figuring out what you really want out of life can be confusing. However, if you approach it from a more practical standpoint, it is not beyond your grasp. You can overcome. You can get out there and meet chicks. But one of the most important aspects of this is, as I've said, the desire to do so. If you'd rather hang out with the guys and watch football, then that's your deal. But if you really want to meet and date women and open up that new world, you can do it. But it does take effort. We all know it's much easier to sit in the recliner with a beer and the remote than it is to get out there and attempt to meet women. But sitting at home isn't going to get you anything but fat and lazy. And, honestly, once you become complacent in this way, not much is going to get you out of the recliner. After that point, everything becomes an effort.

Life takes living and if you make no effort, then you have to realize no one is going to do it for you. I've known a few guys with trust funds who don't do anything with their lives except live off their trusts. They don't work and they don't contribute anything to society. Because of this, they feel useless and have no self-esteem. Sure, they have money but not a lot friends or ladies to hang out with. Why? They don't make an effort. They're content to sit back and let life pass them by. In the end, all they would have to do is apply themselves a little and they'd be in a much happier place.

But once someone becomes content with "the way things are", it's hard to get out of the chair and out there.

"Out there" might mean rejection. Rejection can mean getting hurt and who wants to get hurt? The thing is, getting hurt means you're feeling something and that means you're alive. It means you're trying and no one can fault you for that, not even the person who rejected you. Sitting back and doing nothing means you've stopped living.

Are you content to sit back and let life pass you by? Is this where you are now? Stop and think about it. Do you attempt to go out and meet women? Do you attempt to meet them on internet dating sights? How much effort are you putting into it? If it's little to none, you have to stop right now and ask yourself: *Is this something I even want? Do I really want to start meeting and dating chicks? Can I pull myself out of this chair—out of this life I've created for myself—and find someone to love?*

Maybe you're not looking for someone to love. Maybe you want to play the field a little bit. That's okay too. This is what this book is all about. It's about how to get out there and get it done. But first, you have to be honest and ask yourself if you are willing to make the effort. Because if you're not nothing will work. Chicks won't magically appear in your life. It does take work to meet and date them. And, yes, it does take some money and know-how. And, above everything else, you have to be ready to expend the effort. If you go after it all half-assed, you're more than likely to get rejected, which will make you more gun-shy in the future. But if you go out there and give it your all, you might just surprise yourself and get a big return—a date with a chick you've been dying to go out with.

So, in the end, it is up to you to decide: You have to be interested in dating to want to do it. If you'd rather hang out with your friends, it might not be a good idea to waste your time dating.

The truth about chicks.

One of the most important things to remember is that all not women are alike. Each one is uniquely different. While it's true that they all basically want the same thing—a good man being at the top of the list—it's just that each one will want it at a different time in her life. And each will want to adjust it to her individual preferences.

Once you realize that you can't win them all, you will be better able to get a grasp on what chicks are all about. Don't go into this with the attitude that you can paint every chick with the same brush. If you do that with one, and it works, chances are, the next one will look at you like you're absolutely crazy.

So, do yourself a favor and don't really try to figure chicks out. Sure, you can understand them better and help yourself in that regard but, mostly, trying to gauge what one wants is almost a waste of time. You can't interpret her needs. You can show her a good time and you can be polite, but you can't make her mind up for her. When she wants you to know what she wants, she will most likely tell you. Women aren't shy in this regard.

Remember, each and every woman is an absolute individual. They've all been raised a little differently and each comes from a slightly different background. This means none of them are carbon copies of each other. This is great because it means if one rejects you, another will find you funny and charming. And this is a good thing.

Are you intimidated by chicks?

Don't think this is a trick question. Just ask yourself honestly if you're intimidated by chicks or not. Many, if not all, men are a little intimidated by women. This is because we think they hold the power, the key, to our future happiness. And this is usually before we even speak our first word to them.

Being intimidated by chicks usually means that they just make us very uncomfortable. We're afraid we'll make some sort of flub around them and they'll think we're idiots. And, of course, we're afraid if we have such a flub, they'll reject us or, worse, laugh at us.

Also, being intimidated by chicks usually means that we were probably intimidated by some woman early in our lives. This might sound a bit Freudian, but think about it. If you can locate the source of your intimidation, i.e. your discomfort, you might be able to relieve yourself of it to a certain extent.

So, figure out if perhaps you were intimidated by your own mother or an aunt, teacher, girl next door, etc., when you were younger. Seriously, think about it and don't shrug this off as something silly. Over time, I have come to find out that most problems we have can be traced back somewhere in our psyche. This isn't hocus-pocus or mumbo-jumbo. This is a way to clear your head of the junk inside of it and to move on to a more fulfilling life.

Sometimes, if we are a little intimidated by something, we make it into a bigger monster than it is. We stop looking at things objectively. We also begin to stop looking at women on an individual basis, thusly lumping them all into the "bitches" category, which is a completely wrong thing to do. All it usually means when you do something like this is that you might be a little intimidated by women. They make you uncomfortable for whatever reason.

Keep in mind that most guys are intimidated by many women, even the most confident guys. Most guys dread that first initial meeting. However, what these guys do is get over their intimidation and take a chance, usually with favorable results. They push through the pain, so to speak.

On the other side of this, know that chicks can be intimidated by guys, too. It's just as hard for them to get up and introduce themselves to a guy as it is for the guy. The problem therein, lies in both sexes' inability to get over their intimidation and get on to the business of meeting. It's like we're both waiting for someone to make the first move. And, because men are born with the desire and the cultural expectation to dominate, it's usually left up to them. Fair? Not really, but let's just say, that's life and it's something we have to get over in order to get dates.

So, again, ask yourself if you might be a little intimidated by chicks and be honest. It's really no big deal and even the biggest, toughest guy can be a little scared of women. Figure out why you're intimidated and get over it. Also, you need to know that you're not going to get a woman if you act like a timid little mouse.

Overcoming issues like this before you get out there into the dating scene is going to help you so much. What it means when you work on this stuff is that you leave your baggage behind and don't have to carry it around with you wherever you go. And this makes you more open and receptive to women and can help you get over your fears. And this is a great thing. It also means you'll be ahead of the game when you start.

What kind of guy are you?

There are two kinds of guys in regards to dating. The first is the "man's man" and the second is the "ladies' man". Of course, this doesn't mean there aren't other types of guys out there; we're just talking about dating here. But think about it: Which kind if guy are you?

You need to ask yourself: Do you even *like* women? And, no, I don't mean sexually, I mean as people. This isn't a trick question. I know plenty of guys who don't like to hang out with chicks. They would rather hang out with friends and see a game. They're *men's men*, so to speak. All this means is that they relate better to guys than girls. They're not misogynists or anything; they're just guys who would rather hang out with their friends than try to figure out chicks. They like women but at this point in their lives would rather expend their efforts in another direction—being a guy.

But then, there's another type of guy who's called a *ladies' man*. These guys would rather spend their time "skirt chasing", so to speak. They're not interested in hanging out with their friends too much because they want to get laid. They know there's zero chance of scoring with a chick if all they do is hang out at the sports bar and never meet any chicks. So, they spend most of their time looking to hook-up.

So, which type of guy are you? I'm more of a ladies man, myself but I know lots of guys who are men's men. I think it really is pertinent to figure out which kind of guy you are. Either is fine. It takes all kinds to make the world go around. However, if you're more of a man's man, you need to realize that most women aren't going to be content with a guy who always hangs with his friends. And this may, in fact, be your main problem with women. If you are lucky, you will come across that rare girl who loves sports and games as much as you do. But this isn't likely to happen anywhere other than in some movie.

But it doesn't mean you can't find a fulfilling relationship. It just means you might have to take a different approach to women. You might have to juggle a little more of your time and find a girl who's just as busy with her friends as you are with yours. They do exist but they'll be hard to meet because, like you, they're going to be hanging out with their friends rather than looking for men.

Keep in mind, though, that if you are at the age where most women are looking to settle down and get married, they might not put up with this as much. Women who are ready to nest can be very possessive. They want their man with them at all times, unless he's working, of course. Women do this because if they're considering having babies with you, they need to know you are going to be there to take care of them. If you're always hanging with your friends, she might not want to hang with you at all.

So, if you are the sort of guy who would rather hang out with his friends, just be open and honest from the get-go when you find someone who's just as interested in you as you are in her. If this is something she wants to put up with, she won't have a problem. Just be warned that she might try to change you on down the line and then you will be forced to get your priorities straight. And, yes, women have been known to ask you to choose between her and your friends. So be prepared. The choice and consequences are yours.

I know a lot of guys who would rather hang out with their friends and this is fine. However, it's rare that any of them go on dates—at least not very often—and I doubt if they'll ever get married. But it's what they want and it's what makes them happy, so what does it matter? All that matters is that you figure out what you really want out of life and go from there. It's not written in stone anywhere that you have to get married and procreate. It's not that big of a deal and most everyone isn't going to be that concerned if you don't. However, if you want to make a change in this area of your life, how about trying to strike a balance? You can do this by hanging out with your friend's part of the time and the other times, you can go out and meet women.

On the other hand, if you're a ladies' man, you've already got half the work done. Women love men who love women. It's that simple. And if you love women, it will show. She will know almost from the get-go that you *get* her and that you want to know her. So, she'll be more open to you and to the possibilities you present.

What kind of girl is she?

If we can say that there are two basic types of men—the man's man and the ladies' man—then it would stand to reason that there might also be two types of women. In my experience, I believe this to be true and have found that there are two kinds that predominate.

The types:
- The woman who wants to settle down as soon as possible.
- The party girl who's only concerned about her next night out.

Let me say, firstly, that I am more or less generalizing these two types of women and I do not mean to overlook any other varieties. Because I am generalizing you should know that what I say doesn't apply to each and every woman you might meet and should not be seen as a formula to disparage all women. It's just a way to more or less categorize women so you will know what you are dealing with when you go out. If you can know more about what to expect, you can plan accordingly and expect to have a better time, right?

Let's discuss the first type of woman, the woman who wants to settle down. She might come off as bossier and less fun on the whole than the party girl. The party girl will probably only be looking for a free drink and, if you're lucky, some hot sex later.

With the woman who wants to settle down, she might seem bossy because she's in a hurry. Her biological clock is probably ticking and she doesn't have time for any funny business or game playing. These women are older, usually mid to late thirties or so, although they can be much younger. Regardless, they have no time to party. They're ready to settle down and have a baby. They just have to find a man who's worth having. They're probably more career-oriented than the other type of woman and have spent a great deal of their time getting ahead in the business world. Now it's time to get to the business of husband and babies. If you aren't looking for this as well, get out of her way. Otherwise, if you waste her time, she will be none too pleased.

With the party girl, she's younger, although she can also be much older, and she's just that—a party girl. She wants you to buy her drinks because she's probably not working much and, if she is, it's some crummy job that barely pays the rent. She's not really looking for a commitment from you unless you're so cool you sweep her off her feet. In this case, she'll only stay swept until the party life calls her back, at which point she will turn and run. Don't get too attached to her, though she will be hard not to fall in love with because she will make you love life and living—and partying and drinking. But, like I said, she's probably only in it for a good time and if you start to look a little square to her, she might just cut you loose. Unless, of course, she's really a woman who wants to settle down underneath and the party girl is simply a façade she's built to get you into her clutches. This isn't too likely, but it could be the case in rare instances.

As I've said, these two types of women are generalizations and I mean no disrespect when I say that. Sure, there are other types of women at the club or online to meet. However, be aware that these women are probably vacillating between these two types, the woman who wants to settle down and the party girl. There will be the rare girl just looking to date or for a steady boyfriend, but she might be harder to find as she's probably already been snapped up by some lucky guy.

This isn't to say that other types of women don't exist in the dating world. They do exist and I've comprised a brief list below.

Other types of women in the dating world:
- *The girl who's only looking for Mr. Right, but she'll date Mr. Right Now in the meanwhile.* When Mr. Right comes along, and it's not you, she will dump you in a heartbeat, which can really suck.
- *The girl who's looking for a sugar daddy but will let you buy her dinner sometimes.* In fact, you can buy her anything and even help her with her rent. She may or may not want sex but she will want you to dig deeper into your pocket to help fund her extravagant lifestyle. She's called "high maintenance" for a reason.
- *The single, divorced mom who only wants someone to go out to dinner and have occasional sex with.* She's not interested in a relationship because she just got out of one—a long, drawn-out one. She's a great girl but if you want more than just a steady date, she won't fit the bill. She's probably fun to hang out with, though.

- *The girl who wants to talk about her issues—all night.* She will talk your ear off and, basically, waste your time. She's not interested in dating you, just talking all night about her favorite subject—herself.

- *The girl who's just been cheated on and wants revenge sex, maybe with you.* Of course, don't ever think she'll call you later. She will probably go right back to her boyfriend and torture him by telling him she hooked up with someone—you! Let's hope she doesn't give him your name. (It is probably a good idea to not give this one your full name or any information about where you live.)

- *The seeker girl. This is a girl who wants out of her current relationship but wants someone in his place before she drops the bomb.* She'll be out in the clubs, surveying the room for the "best" pick. And if it's you, be warned that she will want to get right down to business. Keep in mind that she's just replacing one relationship for another. If you're not ready for this kind of quick, short-term commitment, steer clear of her.

- *The married woman.* She's just out with her friends looking for a one-night stand. This sounds like an urban legend, but it does happen, even if it might not ever happen to you. These women want sex and nothing else. Beware of this as you don't want any jealous husbands coming after you. Look for a wedding ring or any talk of kids, mortgages, etc. If you have suspicions that she might be taken, back away from her. It's bad Karma, in my opinion. It can also be quite dangerous to your health.

That pretty much sums it up. Of course, this isn't a concise list and is generalized, as I said, but you get the gist of what I'm saying. Keeping these things in mind will help you to better ascertain situations with chicks as you come across them.

So, be aware of what's going on. Listen to the women you meet and you can usually pick up on which type they are, which will only help you to make a decision right then and there if you want to go ahead with this one or wait it out for your own Mrs. Right.

What most women want. Mostly.

This is hard for any guy to hear but it's something we all have to face at one point or another. Don't freak out. Just listen. It's one of the biggest truths about women. Some guys might say, "Yeah, I knew this already." Some might say, "I figured but hoped it wasn't entirely true." And some might say, "No way!"

Here it is: Most women, even if it's just on a subconscious level, want to eventually get married and have kids. They want a home and security and a man who gives them these things. They will help, of course, by more than likely continuing to work after they're married. And, they want a man who can help with the bills, kids and laundry.

However, on the other hand, there are women who don't want kids. As I said, most women do, but some don't. If they don't, they will probably tell you within the first few dates because these women *really* don't want kids and will not want to date a man who does. This is not to say that these women don't want boyfriends or husbands. But not kids.

But most women do.

And what's so wrong with that? It's a biological imperative, isn't it? You probably want the same thing, too, right? Maybe someday? Of course, you might not want it right now. You may still be a young guy who hasn't gotten on his feet yet. Or maybe you want to play the field before you settle down. That's perfectly fine. It doesn't mean every woman you meet and date is going to want to marry and settle down right this instance, either. It does mean that one day she might want this, whether it's from you or some other guy she meets on down the road.

This is life. This is really what life is all about. It's very grown-up, isn't it? It sounds so serious. But don't let this scare you away from dating. As I said, most men want the same thing women do. It's just they want to sow their world oats, which is fine.

On the other hand, if you do want this right now, there's nothing wrong with it. I know a lot of guys whose main incentive for getting married is to have kids. Some guys I know want kids more than some women, as odd as that may sound. Nothing wrong with it. We're all wired a little differently. But, just don't let this scare you. If you don't want kids, be honest about it from the get-go. There's nothing more horrible than dating someone a while and then finding out you have two totally different life-views.

A way to avoid this is to bring the subject up a few dates in, that is, if you're into this chick and want these things with her. If you're just dating her to be dating her, by no means should you mention kids or marriage. This might give her false hope and then all you have is a big mess and, probably, a horrible breakup. This is where being honest comes in handy.

But knowing things like this from the get-go can help you distinguish the aforementioned woman who wants to settle down right off the bat from the party girl who's only concerned about her next night out. And once you can begin to do that, you can pick which woman you're more comfortable to date. And that puts you more at ease with the whole situation and a little more open to the possibilities of life.

Don't be these guys!

There are certain types of guys that girls hate. If you act like a gentleman and are considerate of others' personal space, you probably won't have a problem with this. However, I wanted to be sure to include this to give everyone a head's up.

One type of guy that women hate the most is the "overbearing guy". You can always spot the overbearing guy in the club who's an embarrassment to all mankind. He's the guy who gets his sights set on one particular girl and focuses all his unwanted attention on her. This means he will glue himself to her side and not leave her alone all night, even if she makes it known she's not the least bit interested in him.

Why does a guy do this? He believes that if he wears this girl down, she'll have sex with him at the end of the night. However, this isn't true. It never works. Also, he's the guy at the club everyone avoids, mainly because his overbearing attitude threatens everyone's good time. You don't want to be this guy!

As we've talked about, rejection is hard, but you should take the first "no" and move on, no questions asked. If you hang around after that, you really do begin to give the chick you're trying to romance the "creep" vibe. Once the "creep" vibe is out, your time with this chick is over. No chick wants to get creeped out by a potential suitor.

This is one of the biggest complaints women have about guys. They complain about the overbearing guy who won't leave them alone. One thing I've figured out by listening to these complaints is the reason *why* chicks are hesitant to be nice to a guy. And the reason is because once they're nice to everyone, some guys take advantage of this and push themselves on them. So, in the end, they have to maintain a distance from most all guys so they don't chance getting stuck with the creepy/pushy guy.

The gist is: If they're not the least bit interested in you, they won't show you *any* interest. And this is because they are afraid they're going to get stuck talking to a creep who won't leave them alone all night.

Does this sound like something you'd like to do? Of course not! So, next time you feel snubbed by a girl, just know that she isn't snubbing you, she's just trying not to get tangled up with a creep all night. And, yes, most chicks are leery of *most* men. That's why you have to take it easy with them at first and not be overbearing and not push yourself on them. This builds trust and once she can begin to trust that you will not be overbearing towards her, she will let you in a little at time.

So, be very aware of how you present yourself to chicks. We all get nervous and sometimes that nervousness makes us appear to be pestering. But being aware of this will help you with your game.

Keep in mind that many chicks have complained about this type of guy over and over. If you grab onto the idea that she might like you if you just "wear her down" and never let go, you might find yourself tossed out of the club. Not only will this really humiliate you, but you'll be forever imprinted on the brain of this one girl as the "creep who wouldn't leave me alone".

It's very important to always act gentlemanly towards women whenever you're around them. All of us have found someone in a club or wherever and just had to have them. It's called physical attraction and that's when we find a girl who is so physically appealing to us that we begin to think they have everything we want. And, while it's perfectly fine to approach a woman like this and introduce yourself, it is far from okay to harass her just because you find her so attractive. You know what? Many other guys find her attractive too.

The only thing you can do in a situation like this is to approach her, say "hello" and let nature take it from there. This is to just see if she might like you, too. If she doesn't like you, no harm, no foul. Then it's okay to excuse yourself and move along.

This is the key to dating well, knowing when to take rejection and move along. That is the smartest thing a guy can do. Believe me, if she doesn't want you at first, she probably never will and so what? There are other girls who will. You just have to find them and by trying, you set yourself up for future success. Because, the more you try, the better you'll get at it.

Keep in mind that you can't get discouraged just because one chick shoots you down! If you do this and go hide under the bed for the rest of your life, what does that prove? Nothing! It's just a form of cowardice. We all get shot down! That's life and if you're going to be a guy who dates and dates well, you have to take the good with the bad. And sometimes the bad is getting rejected. Learn to live with it and get over it as soon as possible. Getting shot down doesn't mean that you've been put out of commission. It means, simply, a bump in the road that you will get over.

Another type of guy that I want to mention and that you should avoid being is the guy who hits on every girl in the club. He goes from one chick to the next, never stopping until one takes the bait. The only problem is, usually no one takes the bait and everyone laughs at him for making such a jerk out of himself. It's okay to be excited, but just don't be too over-eager. This shows desperation and chicks really hate desperation. But then again, you probably hate desperation too, don't you? Everyone does.

One last guy I want to briefly cover is the guy who takes a rejection so personally that he insults the girl. You never want to be the guy who tries to humiliate the girl who's just rejected him. This only makes the situation worse and can give you a bad reputation.

When and if you're rejected, do yourself a favor and always walk away with your head held high. Afterwards, keep going if you get shot down. Never call a girl "bitch" or say anything disrespectful. It really doesn't make her look bad, it makes you look bad—really bad. In fact, you're the one who will ultimately end up looking like a "little bitch". Everyone gets their feelings hurt, but to show it in that way is unacceptable, in my opinion. Personally, I don't want some chick knowing she got to me *that much.* And while it may feel really good in that moment to put her down, just know that being the bigger person doesn't take much and you always come out looking good. So, by walking away without another word, you're showing her you respect yourself too much to make an ass out of yourself and that her rejection isn't going to stop you from having a good time. And do you know what to do then? Go and have a good time! That's the best revenge, hands down.

So, you need to be aware of how you're coming off and strive to be a gentleman at all times. By doing this, you are guaranteeing not being the guy women avoid at all costs. And that puts you in the game more, which can get you better results in the end.

On being a gentleman.

As mentioned briefly in the previous chapter, one of the best things a guy can do on a date or when interacting with women in any way, is to act like a gentleman. Once a guy can do this, he's well on his way to being sought after by many chicks. And once it becomes second-nature, there's no stopping him.

You need to know that most women have, at one time or another, came across jackasses who've either insulted them or treated them like crap. So, it's refreshing to women when they come across a guy who acts like a gentleman. This isn't to say you have to act like some fop from the turn of the century who wears a top hat and carries a cane. It's to say that if you act like a gentleman, you might just get noticed more. And almost every woman out there appreciates a guy who acts like a gentleman.

So, what does a gentleman do? How does he act? This is mostly common sense. You probably already know what being a gentleman entails and mostly it entails being a nice guy who never insults the woman he's with. It's almost like you have to become the bigger person when you're a gentleman. You make others feel comfortable and pay attention to their needs. You ask if they'd like another drink or need anything. It's almost like being a good host at a party you're throwing, though you'll be doing it when you're out looking for women to date and/or on dates. This isn't to say that you should be a push-over. A gentleman is, more or less, a guy who has manners. He's also does various things, as listed below.

A gentleman:
- Always holds the door open for a girl.
- Always pays for drinks and/or dinner.
- Listens to what's being said to him.
- Never insults the person he's with.
- Walks away from a rejection with his head held high.
- Is always the bigger person.
- Doesn't lose his cool.
- Acts graceful in every situation.
- Doesn't let the little things or other people's shortcomings affect his demeanor.
- Is always "smooth".
- Isn't afraid to expand his mind and actually read books on etiquette.
- Isn't afraid to acknowledge that etiquette can help a guy in the dating world.

That is pretty much the gist of it. You may have some ideas of your own about how to be a gentleman and, if so, use them. The point is to know that *the better you act around women, the better you will be perceived*. And what can be better than that?

An important lesson: Don't be overly anxious.

As men, we sometimes get tired of waiting and want to get the show on the road. We want faster computers, cars and video games. We live in a fast-paced world and we like things to happen *now*. However, when it comes to dating, things tend to go a little slower than we'd like. This can sometimes make us overly anxious. And when this happens, we begin to act like we're desperate.

What happens sometimes is that once we zone in on a chick that we really like, we can't wait to get started. We think we have to get right over to her, introduce ourselves and then *make her like us*. We can't wait! We have to do it quickly! It's almost as if we're in a panic, trying to get it done before it's too late. Sure, this just means we're anxious to get on with our lives, but chicks don't operate like that. You have to chill out a little before you thrust yourself on them.

But sometimes we just can't wait. I don't know what gets into our heads but it's like if we don't approach her *right now*, it's going to be too late. It's like this panic takes over us or something. Maybe we're afraid some other guy will beat us to it and he'll get the girl we really want. Maybe we're afraid she might leave before we make our move. Whatever the reason, what we need to do is calm down and take our time. Being overly anxious is not a good thing when it comes to meeting or dating chicks. It can make us look and act like fools.

So, take a breath and listen to this: Never be too overly anxious to meet or date any chick. Being overly anxious makes women think you are this thing they despise: Desperate. If she thinks you're desperate, then that will make her very uncomfortable. And if she's uncomfortable, she's going to pull away right to begin with. This means you will have no chance with her.

But think about desperation objectively for a moment. Most of us don't like desperation in any form. It makes us uncomfortable. Have you ever been to a furniture store and had a desperate salesperson follow you around? How does it make you feel? Uncomfortable? Yes, it does! All you want is for this guy to leave you alone so you can shop around without having someone looking over your shoulder the whole time. It's just plain annoying, isn't it? It might even make you set your jaw to resist buying anything regardless of how well you like it.

So, would it not stand to reason that if you come off as overly anxious/desperate, it might make a woman uncomfortable and/or annoyed? Yes, of course, it does. It might even strengthen her resolve *not* to like you.

What a woman needs when she first meets a new guy is to feel comfortable. And most of them know that guys are trying to get into their pants. This is universally true. Sure, you could ask why this doesn't make them feel flattered to know guys want "some of that", but think about it. What if you had a total stranger pushing themselves into your personal space and then looking at you like you're on display? It makes you feel like a piece of meat, right? And that's how they feel when this happens. It doesn't make them feel flattered or sexy. It makes them downright suspicious. They think— *Why is this guy so desperate to talk to me? Is there something wrong with him? He must not have anything going on in his life. Man, what a creep!* You become the furniture salesman she desperately wants to get away from. Once she categorizes you like that, you're toast. And all you have to do avoid it is to not become overly anxious.

This is one of the main reasons why most women have their defenses up right off the bat. Becoming intimate with someone is an idea that takes a while to warm up to. They're not just going to hand it over, especially not if someone makes them feel uncomfortable. They only want to give it up once they know they can totally trust a new person. Women need to be able to trust you, as a man. Why? Because if they get half-way into sex and change their mind—which they can and will do, believe me—they want to know you'll back off and not give them a hard time about it. They want to know that you're not some kind of creep or stalker. And that you'll let them off the hook without a guilt trip.

Another thing, desperation makes you stupid. It really clouds your head and makes you do stupid things like hound a girl for her number or to buy her a drink. After you ask the first time and she declines, do yourself and your ego a favor and walk away. Because, if not, you will look back at an incident like this and inevitably ask yourself, "What was I thinking?"

It happens to the best of us, believe me.

Plus, if you're overly anxious, she's going to think you're some kind of spaz. You want her to have the best possible impression of you right off the bat. First impressions do have the most impact and it is hard to recover from a bad first impression. So, do yourself a big favor and only approach a chick when you're ready to be calm and not desperate.

The number one secret to getting the girl.

I'm about to share a valuable piece of information that took me years to realize. You really should be sitting down for this one. Are you ready? Here goes...the number one secret to getting the girl:

The guy that gets the girl is the guy that makes the move.

I put it in bold for a reason. I want this to sink in. Did you read it? Does it make sense? It's so simple that most guys overlook it. Or, they're looking for an excuse not to make a move out of fear of rejection. But this is so true, I can't believe how many guys don't know it. And I can't stress how important it is for you to understand this.

Have you ever seen a very average looking guy with a knockout girl? Of course, you have. You've probably seen them on sitcoms and in real life as well. You think—"Well, he must have a lot of money." Not usually. You think—"He must be a scam artist to get a girl like that and probably fed her a good line of BS." Not necessarily.

So, what did he do to get this beautiful girl? Hypnosis? A love potion? How?! He asked, that's how. He wasn't too intimidated to go after the good looking woman. Learn from this guy and stop being intimidated!

I know plenty of really good looking women that date and go on to marry these guys—these average, everyday Joes. Why? Because many of them want to get married and have kids, someday. They can't wait forever for the perfect guy. And they can't wait forever for guys to get the nerve to approach them, either.

Keep in mind that many women aren't just looking for looks when they're out to date. Most of them are not that shallow. Looks seems to be way more important to men than they are to women. It's true. I know this from personal experience. We get upset if we know women are interested in looks, but most of the time, we're looking for the beautiful buxom blonde, right?

Most women are looking for a guy who wants to settle down and help take care of them. They're looking for a possible father for their unborn kids. They're looking for someone to vacation with, to take them on dates, to give them Valentine's gifts.

That guy could very well likely be you. You don't believe me, do you? Why not? I've seen it happen time and time again. Sure, some guys get the girl by pulling scams by pretending to be virgins or artists or millionaires or whatever. But many guys don't have to resort to these pathetic tactics. They, simply, have enough confidence to ask a girl out that they like. And they don't let some chick's good looks stop them. If they like the girl, they're going to ask her out, no questions asked. She might very well turn them down but that doesn't matter because they don't care if she turns them down. Know why? Because they know they're going to develop a rapport with her and she will eventually come around. They do this by being nice and excusing themselves after the first rejection. Then, the next time they see her, they give her a casual, "Hey, how are you?" When they say this, they give her a smile that disarms her and, usually, if she doesn't have anything lined up to do, she figures, "What the hell? Why not give him a chance? He's nice enough."

Please note that these guys do not harass or "wear down" these women. They just let them know they're available when and if they like. Also, they know if one doesn't work out, someone else will, so what do they have to lose? Nothing, that's what.

You ask—"Why? Why would this hot chick go out with this average guy with an average car and an average job? She can do better." I know you're thinking this because I thought this until I figured it out and tried it for myself. But just think about it as it's mostly common sense.

If you haven't noticed, there aren't that many millionaires hanging on trees waiting for beautiful women to pick them. These guys travel in different circle and usually only meet women in their social circle. And not every beautiful woman in the world is in these guys' social circles. Besides that, there are a lot of people in the world today— over a billion! Not every guy that gets a beautiful babe has the opportunity to win the lottery or become a successful movie producer. And that means not every beautiful girl can afford to sit around and wait for one of these guys to show up.

I'll tell you how I came across this important piece of information. I was watching a late-night talk show and there was a popular, beautiful young actress being interviewed. The subject of prom came up and the host asked the actress who she went to prom with. She told him, "No one. I never got asked." He was flabbergasted and said, "What is it with these guys who never ask these beautiful girls out?" And I thought to myself, "He's right. If you don't ever ask, how can a guy expect to date someone like that?" I went out the next night and put this information to use. And, invariably, my world opened up.

You see, most women are waiting for a guy to make a move. Regardless of the effects of the women's movement, this is the way it works in our society. They're waiting on someone to ask them as many women are just as shy as guys and fear rejection as much as they do. And, since they're women, they figure the guy *should* make the first move. And you know what? He should. Sure, some guys get lucky and have women falling all over them. But if you'll notice, it's usually not the beautiful girls doing the fawning.

So, there you go. There is the secret to getting the girl.

This is why it is so important to be ready to ask one of these women out. That's why you shouldn't hesitate to get into shape and have a nice outfit or two on hand when the opportunity presents itself. Because, when you realize this, your eyes will open and you will understand that these opportunities are all around. You just have to be ready for them.

So, whenever you see a beautiful woman and want to ask her out, don't tell yourself you don't have a chance. Just ask yourself, "What do I have to lose?" You never know, you might get lucky. And keep in mind that many attractive women complain that they don't get asked out that much. Why? Because most guys are too intimidated to ask them out for fear they'll get shot down. Now that you know this, what do you have to lose? You never know, that beautiful girl might just be waiting on you to make that first move.

Also, think of it like this: You might be the only guy who has the nerve to ask this hot woman out. Think about that and the effect it could have on both of your lives.

You have to have confidence.

I've discussed this briefly several times over the last few chapters but I thought it would be beneficial to dedicate a whole chapter to this one subject—confidence.

Confidence is important in anything you do in life. Whether it's asking a girl out on a date, interviewing for a job or taking a test, confidence matters. Without confidence, it's hard to muster up the courage to go through with anything. Without confidence, a guy stays a boy and never transforms into a man. He stays at a very immature level because that's where he feels no pain. Without feeling a little pain, you never experience growth and if you never experience growth, you can never hope to get that chick or turn into a man.

A guy with confidence doesn't have to the best looking guy in the room because it doesn't matter. He's got the confidence to approach most any woman and talk to her. Why? Because he doesn't worry about getting shot down. He worries about missing out on his chance to talk to a babe. And if she doesn't respond favorably, it's her loss, not his.

If you don't have much confidence, it is absolutely pertinent that you get some. A guy without confidence can be a painful thing. You have to realize that no one is really going to build you up and give you that confidence you lack. It has to come from within. You have to call it up and learn how to use it.

So, how do you do this? How you gain some confidence? It's easy. *You become the best version of you that you can be.* That includes doing any self-improvement you have to do to get yourself up there with the rest of the confident men.

But the most important aspect of all of this is knowing that you are worth it. You are worth a second look and you're worth some chick talking to. Every guy is! You have to believe you are the best and that you can get the best woman out there—and all you have to do is make the effort.

Building your confidence doesn't take much. You don't have to do daily self-affirmations in the mirror each morning telling yourself how great you are. All you have to do is get out there and try. And if you get shot down? You keep trying until you don't get shot down. You do this without being pushy or making a fool out of yourself. You can also pretend to be confident until you *become* a confident guy— just fake it until you make it, as they say.

As with anything, there's no gain without pain. It's hard to get out there and let those girls know you're alive. It's hard to go up to one and introduce yourself. But you know what? Without doing it, you stay stuck and then you get bitter.

So, get some confidence. It's inside of you and you can bring it out. As I've said, all you do to bring it out is try. And if you fail? Try, try again until you succeed as that's what really builds confidence. That's really all there is to it.

Don't be afraid to fail!

Most successful people have one thing in common—they got over their fear of failure. Whether it was to open their own business or move to another country, people who succeed in life try. Failing is part of trying and if you don't try, you fail without even making an attempt at something. In essence: If you don't try, you automatically fail—at anything you do.

It's that simple. You have to try in order to succeed. This is one of the most important messages in this book—get out there and give it a shot! Just try it! See what happens! Don't be afraid to fail!

You have to keep in mind that it's okay to fail. We live in a country where it seems as though failing is the worst possible thing you could ever do. But if this were true, there would probably never be any "new and improved" items on the market or any divorced people remarrying. Failure is a must to life because failure lets us know what we're doing wrong and how we can improve. Failure is our guidepost to the future.

So, when you start going out and dating, keep this in mind. It might take you a few tries to meet a girl who says "yes" to going out with you. This is okay! Don't despair! Just keep trying. And, sure, it might take you a few tries after that to get a second date with some of the chicks you take out. This is okay, too! Who cares? It means you're trying and, along with trying, will soon come success. If it doesn't work with one chick, go onto the next and to the next until it works! Someone will eventually respond favorably.

Guys who finally win the girl they want keep trying. Guys who want to get married and have kids have to date a few women before they find one they are compatible with. Guys who want to play the field have to get out there in the bars and clubs and establish a network. It's all about trying and doing what works.

So, don't be afraid to fail. Because if you are, you will never even try. And that will get you nowhere.

Chicks need finessing.

If you want to please a woman, you have to learn how to finesse her a little. If she looks at you as the kind of guy who really wants to please her, she'll want to please you.

By "finessing" I simply mean, show her a little respect, open the door for her, wait for her to sit first and ask her if she'd like wine with the meal. Stuff like that which is so simple but many guys overlook by being too nervous. This is finessing her and being a gentleman, as we discussed in a previous chapter. This is showing her that you are listening to her needs and taking care of them. This will make her respect you and want to keep you around for a while.

As I said, some guys just get too nervous when they first go out. All you have to do is take a breath and think about what you're doing. Soon, it will come as second nature.

Here's a list of how to finesse her:
- Open the door.
- Wait for her to sit first.
- Ask her what she'd like to drink.
- Really listen to what she's saying and respond accordingly.
- Be respective of her personal space and never lean over and touch her unless she does it to you first.

- Know a few good, clean jokes to tell. If they're lame or you don't get a laugh, just shrug it off with a, "I'm not good at telling jokes". She might see this as vulnerability and think you're cute.
- Bring her a small bouquet of flowers or box of nice candies when you meet for that first date. This shows her that you were really looking forward to seeing her and that you appreciate her taking the time.
- Don't correct her if she misspeaks or speaks too loudly. She's probably nervous herself and that's how it's coming out.

Of course, there are other ways in which you can finesse chicks. You may have a few ideas of your own. The key here is to know when to hold back so you don't feel as though you are groveling or making a fool out of yourself. Doing little things is what you're after. You don't want to bake her a cake or buy her a piece of expensive jewelry right off the bat. You just want to show yourself to be a stand-up guy who is willing to go the extra mile for a girl he likes. This is, more or less, just acting like a gentlemen. It shows the girl you're with that you can hold back but you can also prove yourself to be date-worthy as well.

For some guys, this stuff comes as second-nature. They were taught this stuff as kids. Those are the lucky ones, right? Most of us haven't got a clue about these little things that mean so much to chicks. However, by becoming aware of how going the extra mile from time to time can lead to a more meaningful, intimate relationship with a girl, a guy can really shine in this department. The great thing about it is that once you start doing it for one girl, it will become second nature and then the other girls you meet and date will appreciate you as well.

Also, keep in mind that just because the women's movement happened, doesn't mean it's okay for guys *not* to have to do this kind of stuff. I know this may come off as sounding ridiculous, but I know some guys who think that the equal rights movement means they don't have to put the effort out. Equal rights don't mean she turned into a man, you know? It just means she has better access to better pay and that means it has nothing to do with the dating world. If you find yourself thinking like this, get over it. It's just an excuse for you not to be considerate. Learning the truth about things like this and accepting it will save you so much trouble, and, quite possibly, keep you from making a fool of yourself in the future. On a date, women like to be treated like women, not one of the guys.

Turn-offs for chicks.

As we all know, chicks can be very picky. Some chicks won't go out with you if you don't have the "right" stuff—in other words, the right shoes, car, house, etc. And there are some chicks won't look at you if you don't look like a movie star. But most chicks, generally, aren't that picky. However, there are universal things that turn them off, especially within the first few minutes or hours of meeting you.

Chicks really don't like:
- Bad hygiene and that includes ratty nails, hair or clothes.
- Bad manners. Sure, she might belch in front of you, but it's not likely. Make sure you don't belch or pass gas in front of her—even if she does it trying to be funny or daring. She might laugh at herself for doing something like this but she will find it disgusting if you do it. If you do so accidentally, apologize and then change the subject quickly.
- Bragging. Unless you can really back it up, don't brag about anything. It rarely impresses anyone and it is usually a sign of insecurity.

- Drunks. If you're slurring your words, don't approach a chick. Get some coffee and a ride home from a buddy.
- Loud-mouths. These guys are so loud everyone looks at them in annoyance. Just try to keep your voice at a normal level.
- Gropers. Any guy who tries to pat a woman's butt will more than likely get nothing but a slap across the face. Being too "handsy" or touchy-feely is not a good idea either. It doesn't matter if you're "Italian" or have "old world sensibilities, either. You will only make her uncomfortable. It's hands off until she gives you the greenlight.
- Disrespect. Some guys lose it when they get rejected and start yelling expletives at the girl who's just done the rejecting. Or they might just be disrespectful in general. These guys are never going to land a woman because they don't know how to treat a woman.
- Inquisitive jerks. These are the guys who want to talk to a girl about sex, her shaving habits, etc.— all within a few hours of meeting her. You should never ask her these things unless you are in a solid, dating relationship, and certainly not just after you meet.
- Corrective guys. These guys take it upon themselves to correct a woman's pronunciation or how she holds a fork, etc. Sure, after you've been dating, if she has a problem, point it out in a kind, sensitive way. But never on a first date.
- Cursers. Don't curse in front of her at first. Just don't. It looks bad. If she curses? Overlook it would be my advice, or she might start cursing

you. She might think of her foul mouth as being edgy. On you, she might find it obnoxious.

- Guys who try too hard to be funny. These guys tell the same corny jokes over and over again during the date in hopes of disarming their date. Or they make "funny" noises like animals sounds or talk in different accents, in a lame attempt to look like a comedian. They usually just come off looking like jackasses.

These are just the basics that you should be aware of. Of course, most guys aren't going to go out and make a jerk out of themselves on purpose. It's just something that happens sometimes because of nerves or awkward silences. If you do make a blunder, however, don't let it stop you. Just apologize and try to change the subject. Don't agonize over any mistakes because she may think you're too intense. Be aware that some chicks won't call you on bad behavior. They'll just give you an icy stare and vow to never see you again. That is, if you're lucky, because that way you'll know to apologize. But most likely, they'll pretend that nothing's wrong, which will give you false hope, and then they'll ignore your calls. So, if this happens and you wonder later why she won't take your call, think back to see if you might have made a blunder. If so, let it go and just try to do better next time.

This is true of most chicks.

Chicks really *are* looking for a reason to turn you down. Whether it's when you first meet them, go on your first date or whatever. This is because most of them were brought up by protective fathers and mothers who taught them that men are only out for one thing—to get laid. So, from the get-go, most chicks are on their toes and looking for a reason not to get involved with you. They might not be conscious of it, but most of them are mentally "saving themselves" for the "right guy".

Sure, there are exceptions, such as like when she's interested in you first or whatever. But, mostly, women have to feel you out before they make a commitment whether to date you or even let you talk to them. This is also in part due to the aforementioned pushy guys who, if they give the slightest bit of interest, won't leave them alone. However, when it's you being rejected, you tend to think it's because she's just, simply, a bitch. However, this isn't the case. She's just trying to protect herself.

Let me put it this way: If a chick isn't really interested in you, she's not going to be. So, if you walk over and stink or are too drunk to talk, she's *really* not going to be interested. You're just embarrassing yourself. So, why push it? I wouldn't.

Dating costs money.

One of the biggest complaints I hear from guys is that dating is too expensive. We do live in an expensive world, there's no doubt, and chicks like to be treated well. This includes buying her dinner and drinks.

The best thing to do in this situation is to just accept this as part of dating. If course, if you are in college or just starting out, the women you'll be dating will be more tolerate of going Dutch. They'll probably give you some slack in this area and be understanding. However, if you're really interested in dating someone seriously, asking them to buy their own dinner is a good way to insure you *won't* be dating her seriously.

It's not that women expect you to go broke taking them out to dinner. They just want to know that you're interested enough in them to pay. Regardless of the women's movement, most women are old-fashioned in a lot of respects and this is no exception. They expect to have their dinner bought for them. If you really want a serious relationship with someone, one way to kill it right off the bat is to ask her to buy her food.

I know many guys don't have loads of money to spend on chicks and that's fine. But why not try saving a bit here and there and have it on hand when you meet that special one? Showing her that you like her enough not to ask her to buy her own meal lets her know that you think she's special enough for this and that she can trust you. Without trust, there won't ever be anything else. You have to give her a reason to grab onto you. If there's nothing to grab onto you—you don't buy her dinner or whatever—there's no real reason for her to date you.

Something else to consider is this: Don't ever expect sex in exchange for dinner. Sounds ridiculous, but I've known guys who've complained that they spent money on a girl "for nothing". Never go into a dinner date thinking it will lead to sex.

However, like I said earlier, if you're in college and on a limited budget, you might get away with going Dutch. Yet, if you really like a chick, try to pay for everything—drinks, dinner, movies, etc. If you can't afford to, like I said, why not save up some money until you can? You don't want to look cheap to a chick you really like. The point of paying is that if you really like her and want to pursue her, this will give her one less reason *not* to reject you. But if you're just going out with her in order to get laid, just know one meal isn't going to cut it.

So, what if you are a guy who wants to date but can't really afford it? What can you do? Most dating, as we all know, is a movie and dinner. That's just the standard. But if you can't afford it, you will have to use your imagination. Try some new things, like walks on the beach if you live near one or cooking for her at your place. You can probably think of a thousand things to do where you two can be alone to interact and get to know each other.

But otherwise, just cough up the cash and hope for the best. Sure, you might spend a hundred bucks on a date that comes to nothing. But if you look at it like that, why are you even attempting to date? Like I said before, what you need to do is look at it as an experience, not as something that's going to make or break you, financially or otherwise. It's something you are doing in order to get out of the house, have a good time and look for a potential mate. And, that means spending a few bucks. So what? Like I said, if you've got it to spend, spend it and if you don't, just save up until you do. You don't want to embarrass yourself—or her.

However, as I mentioned, no chick expects you to go broke on her. Have your limit of what you can spend, if you must, and pick a place that you can afford. It's not that hard to do. There's lots of places to go that don't cost that much. Also, why not go to the movies during matinee time?

But if you can afford to spend the cash and you want to impress a chick, do so. She'll be flattered and that will earn you points and maybe a second date.

If she likes you...really, really likes you...

Anything you do is probably not going to turn her off. If you're lucky enough to find a chick like this right off the bat, that is. As I said, most chicks are looking to turn guys down right from the get-go for whatever reason. But, sometimes, fortune does indeed shine upon us and we meet the right one, right off the bat.

If so, count your lucky stars. That is, if you like her, too.

Don't take rejection personally.

Rejection, rarely, has much to do with the person who's been rejected. I've come to realize this over time. Rejection, a lot of the time, says more about the person doing the rejecting than the rejected.

Regardless, it sucks, it really, really does. Rejection feels horrible to everyone. It makes us feel small and humiliated and just terrible. It can make us miserable, if we let it. Unchecked, it can turn us bitter and sad.

But it doesn't have to. As I said, rejection is more than likely not about you. So, you shouldn't take it so hard or put so much into it. It's about what's going on with her. There are multitudes of reasons why a chick might reject you and the least of it has to do with you. Sure, you may not have what she's looking for. That could be true. And if that's the case, by her rejecting you, she's just saved you a lot of trouble and probably some heartache.

No one can take the sting of rejection away. You have to feel it, so feel it and walk away with your head high. You've done nothing but try, so pat yourself on the back for giving it a shot.

So, why is she rejecting you?

Reasons she might reject you:
- She might be involved already.
- She might be nursing a broken heart.
- She might be a lesbian.
- She might hate men in general.
- She might have baggage.
- She might have chemical dependency issues.
- You might just not be her type.

If you look this list over, you will obviously see that none of these reasons have anything to do with you. So, don't take rejection so personally. Keeping these things in mind before you approach a chick can help you to get over some of your nervousness. (Obviously, keep in mind that there may be other reasons, too, that don't fall on this list.) Just tell yourself if she rejects you, it's probably because of one of these reasons. It's time to put yourself out there and get going and if you get hung up on personal issues—like thinking chicks will always reject you for whatever reason—then you'll never date.

So, just know that trying is the hardest thing to do. Putting yourself out there is hard. But if you get a date with someone you really like, it will be worth a little pain, discomfort and embarrassment. And, yes, expect to be embarrassed at first until you get your footing. It takes practice and if you put yourself out there and practice, you will be ahead of the game and it will get easier over time.

Does she have baggage?

This chapter ties in a little with the previous one—reasons why she might reject you. The difference here is that you won't know about her baggage until after you're on a date, or even later, after you or she decides you're not right for one another and stops calling.

When you first go out with a chick, you don't know what she's bringing to the table. She might have all kinds of baggage that you just don't want to deal with. Unfortunately, you usually won't know about this baggage until after you're seated in a restaurant and can't leave quickly.

There's no way to tell if the object of your affection has baggage, unless, of course, it's so obvious that you disregarded the idea of dating her from the get-go. Having baggage, for anyone, means that their relationships will be somewhat tainted from the get-go. But, what, exactly, does baggage entail? There are many issues a chick could be carrying around with her, but for the sake of brevity, I'll just hit the high spots.

The most common source of baggage is, in my opinion, a broken heart. She may have just broken up with what she thought was the "love of her life". Unfortunately, in this case, she might be dating you on the rebound. If so, you won't know until she's probably bounced you. Common elements, however, is if she keeps talking about an ex or a broken engagement. Or, she keeps saying, "Well, my last boyfriend…" If this happens, all I can say is I feel for you, dude, I really, really do. And, no, you can't just leave in the middle of dinner. So, sit back, listen and at the end of the night, just tell her, in the nicest way possible, "Sorry, I think you might still have feelings for your ex." She should get the hint and maybe, on her next date, will use a little more discretion.

The next most common source of baggage is kids. The girl you like and want to date may have one or two or more. If so, she might bring a little guilt along with the date, depending on the kids' ages, as the younger they are, the more guilt she might have for being out with you instead of staying at home with them. If this happens, just assure her that she deserves a break from the kids occasionally and tell her, if she likes, that in the future, you can include them on one of your dates. That is, if you like and want kids around. If you find out "too late" that she's got kids and that's not your scene, just continue on the date but at the end of the night, be honest with her and tell her you're not ready for that kind of commitment. There's nothing wrong with it as many guys aren't ready and you shouldn't give her any wrong ideas. But, if you don't mind kids, encourage her to talk about them or show you their pictures she's sure to keep in her wallet.

Another source of baggage might not be so common. This baggage might be that she's confused about her sexual orientation. She might be bi-sexual or think that she might be a lesbian. If this is the case, sorry, man. Sometimes life is funny. Just overlook it and chalk it up to a life experience.

The next might be that she's in financial dire straights. Her money problems may be weighing heavily on her mind. This chick could be up to her eyeballs in debt and have creditors calling her at all hours. This is probably more common than you think as women these days go into debt for clothes, cars and anything else without much thought about what it's doing to their financial future. If she wants to talk about this, just sit back and listen. Maybe you know about finances and can offer her some good advice. However, if she asks you for a loan, be wary and don't do it. I don't know many chicks who would stoop this low, but desperate situations call for desperate measures. So, be aware.

Along this vein, the chick you're with might be in the process of being downsized from her job or afraid she's about to get fired.

Another one is that she might have a health problem she's concerned about. With this, it's unlikely she'll let you in on it within hours of meeting you, unless it's really bothering her. If she does talk about it, just sit back and listen and offer her kind words. Or, she might be concerned about a family member with a health problem.

These are just a few common sources of baggage. Being aware of things can help you better ascertain a situation. It might be the reason she's not responding to your conversation. If you find that she's seems disinterested or distracted, just stop for a moment and ask if there's anything bothering her and would she like to talk about it. Be prepared, though, as this might open the floodgates, including tears. If this happens, just listen attentively and don't try to find the nearest exit. If you really like this girl and want a relationship with her, listening like this will help you two form a bond and she will begin to trust you.

A lot of the time we guys seem to see women as having the world on a string and no problems. We view them almost on a pedestal, free from worry and baggage. However, they do have problems. They do have baggage. None of us go through life unscathed. So, being understanding of her situation might open the door for a deeper intimacy than you ever imagined.

Mutual nervousness.

When you first meet someone you're attracted to, you're nervous, right? Some people get nervous meeting anyone new, whether they want to pursue a romantic relationship with them or not.

Well, most chicks are the same way. They get just as nervous as you do when they zone in on a new guy. Biologically, if she's unattached, she's looking for a potential partner in most guys she meets. She's probably unaware that she's even doing this. But so what? Guys are doing the same thing. It's called biological imperative, which simply means that we're all looking for that special someone to meet, hook up with and, possibly mate with.

Of course, this is all done on a subconscious level, so never walk up to a girl and ask if she finds your genes attractive. That's not just corny, that's stupid.

However, it's good to be aware that most chicks are nervous when they're approached by a guy. Usually, they know you're interested, otherwise, why would you be talking to them? Don't let this deter you, though. Just follow through. That's all it takes. Remember that they're human beings too so they understand that this comes with the territory.

Awkward silences and how to avoid them.

Ah, we all know about those awkward silences. These are the times during the first meeting or first date where the conversation just dries up. We then begin to panic, wondering what to say next but nothing comes to mind. We begin to grapple with ourselves, trying to come up with something to say and, of course, a blank forms in our minds.

Is there anything more uncomfortable? Well, yeah, there are lots of things that are more uncomfortable but not many that can occur during a first date. Does it mean that we don't have anything in common with this chick and that we might as well give up? Of course not. It simply means that we've just met someone new and we haven't yet developed any common interests with her.

So, what can you do? How can you avoid those awkward silences? Like I said, you have to develop some commonalties with this girl. And all you have to do is simply inquire—without being too nosey—about her likes and dislikes. After she says, for instance, that she likes a certain team, you can tell her about your favorite team or television show, etc.

The point is to get her talking, then you can respond and, hopefully, avoid those awkward silences. If you draw a blank, try to remember a few things from the list below that can help pull you out of an awkward silence.

Some things you can talk about:
- Where she went to school—high school, college, etc.
- Television shows, movies, all forms of entertainment, including video games.
- If she drinks—what's her favorite drink.
- Her favorite food. (Don't be surprised of course, if it's chocolate.)
- Her parents and siblings and how they can drive her mad.
- Her nieces or nephews. (For that matter, she may have kids of her own and might want to talk a little about them.)
- Her future plans. (This doesn't include dating you right now. Just if she plans on returning to school, getting into a different career, etc.)
- Her favorite music.
- And, if all else fails, compliment her on her outfit and ask her where she got it.

There are many more subjects and I am sure you can think of a few yourself. The point is to keep the conversation flowing without becoming overbearing or appearing too over-eager.

As mentioned earlier, always keep in mind that chicks are just as nervous as you are about meeting or dating someone for the first time. So, if you show confidence and interest, you will help her to feel a bit more comfortable and, when that happens, both of you can relax and have a good time.

Why do chicks seem to love jerks?

Some guys have asked me, "Why is it some guys can be absolute jerks and chicks fall all over them? How can they treat a girl like crap and still have her like them?" The answer is simple: Chicks love jerks. It's always been this way and probably isn't going to change any time soon. But why? It's a human conundrum that can only be summed up like this: We seem to only really like and want those who seem to care nothing for us.

Wrap your head around that piece of information and let it sink it. However, don't take it at face-value because if you act cocky with a girl you better have something to back it up with. This is the truth and it hurts, but if you bring nothing to the table, you can't get away with acting like a jerk.

So, how can some guys act like jerks and get away with it? Because these guys have something extra that they're bringing to the table that many of us don't have. In essence, they have what it takes to act like a jerk.

What you need to act like a jerk:
- A fat bank account, as in lots of money and the willingness to spend it.

- A position of power in the entertainment industry—producer, entertainer, director, up and coming artist, etc. Or a position of power within politics, as in being a member of congress, etc.
- A degree in medicine or law.
- Looks. Sorry, but you need to look like a movie star or at least the poor cousin of one to act cocky.
- A place in a successful or up and coming rock band.
- Loads of confidence.

These are the main things a guy needs to act like a jerk. It usually takes looks, money or power for a guy to be able to get away with acting like a jerk. Women are intrigued by guys like this and are and innately drawn to them. In my opinion, it's the exact same thing as guys do when they "chase" a beautiful girl and "have to have her". Men just seem to be drawn towards certain types of women. So, can you fault a chick for doing the same thing?

Women, like men, want what they can't have and if they think some guy doesn't like them, they want him to like her, so, perhaps, they can get back in the power position by using their womanly wiles. What most women don't understand is that a jerk isn't going to ever allow her to get in the power position. He's not going to be easily whipped, that's for sure. And that's why women keep chasing them— they're a challenge.

So, if you're not a rich lawyer or whatever, what can you do with this knowledge? You can take this vital piece of information and use it to your advantage, that's what. This is where confidence comes in so handy. If you have confidence you don't have to be cocky. Chicks, many times, misinterpret cockiness for confidence. So, whenever you're around a chick you like, you can let her know you're interested but don't ever fawn over her. Give her enough attention to let her know you're alive but never enough to think you're trying to "do something". Keeping a nice distance will work to your advantage by allowing her to size you up and see that you have confidence and could basically take her or leave her. If a chick thinks you don't need her, she might want to start needing you.

Do you get what I'm saying? While being a jerk might work for some guys, for most it makes them seem like— well, jerks. You never want to get on a chick's bad side by treating her like crap in an effort to make her like you. You want to intrigue her enough with your confidence so that she'll want to know more about you. That's the goal. Give it a try and see how well it works.

Meeting and dating chicks.

Now that you've begun to work on yourself and getting your confidence together, it's time to turn to the actual part of meeting and dating chicks. This part, in and of itself, is very simple and straightforward. It shouldn't be hard for you to pick up on it and do your best.

But keep in mind that you have to have a desire to do this. You have to want to meet and date chicks. And it is entirely up to you to get out there and get into the game.

Also, remember that all you're doing to yourself is simple tweaking. You are not going to have to overhaul your entire personality. You are just trying to gain some confidence and you do that by making sure you look the best you can before going out. Body and clothes are important to keep neat and clean because no chick wants a slob. If she sees that you have it together, she won't judge you harshly. She will, more than likely, want to know what's up with you.

Having said all that, let's move on to the good stuff—getting you out there to meet and date chicks.

Where in the world are you going to meet her?

Before you can begin to meet a chick, let alone date one, you have to locate some first, that's a given. So, where are all the chicks? They're everywhere, that's where! They're at the mall, in grocery stores, in the clubs. They're working as waitresses, in your office. They're out there the same as you, living life. But where should you go to find one?

Places you might meet available chicks:
- At a barbeque, party, company picnic.
- At a park.
- At the zoo.
- At the club.
- At the post office or any public building.
- At the bookstore or video store or anywhere you might browse before buying.
- At restaurants.
- At the dog park.
- At church.
- Wherever people congregate.

That's most everywhere you go, isn't it? That's the point! Chicks are everywhere and, usually, they're available.

Some aren't though and you should never approach a chick unless you are fairly certain she's available otherwise you're just going to receive an avoidable rejection. It might be hard to tell.

She might be unavailable if:
- She's got a few kids with her.
- She's got a wedding band or engagement ring on.
- She's with her friends.
- She's holding hands with another chick.

Also, just so you'll know, if she's scowling or looking really disagreeable, she probably doesn't want to be approached by anyone, so stay away. She might be PMSing and ready to snap someone's head off. Don't be that guy without his head. Let some other guy test the waters and suffer the fate.

How to approach a chick.

So, you're ready. You've got the clothes, your body is in good shape and you've showered and shaved. You smell good and want to get to the business of finding a girl. You want to get it done so the nervousness can subside and you can get on with your life.

Relax! This is supposed to be fun! Don't take it so seriously and keep in mind that if you get shot down, there's lots of other fish in the sea. This is the most important lesson this book can teach you: Get over your fear of rejection and relax! This isn't brain surgery; it's just talking to a chick.

But there's an important thing you need to do before you do anything. Before you approach a chick, assess the situation. Each chick will be different and you need to figure out what exactly you want from this woman you're about to talk to.

What, exactly, do you want to do?
- Do you want to buy her a drink?
- Do you want to start a conversation, just to talk?
- Do you want to ask her on a date?

Whatever you want to do is fine. You might talk to a chick and then decide she isn't right for you and that's okay. But before you approach, have an opening ready and something to say so you won't get all tongue-tied. The best opening line? "Hello." It's really that simple. Just say, "Hello, how are you?" When she responds, ask her a question such as, "Are you having a good time?" However, if you meet her at work or whatever, you can ask what floor she works on, who's her supervisor or something work-related. You will have to tweak all this for each situation.

Keep in mind that you will be nervous but that's okay. Don't let this deter you! Practice makes perfect and the more you do this, the better you'll get at it. Sometimes, you might get lucky and she'll let you know it's okay to approach her. And, if this happens, how will you know she's interested in you?

How to tell if she's interested:
- She'll smile at you.
- She'll act a little shy.
- She'll stare at you then look away when you stare back.
- She gives you a signal to approach her such as tossing her hair or motioning you over.

If she does this, most of your work is already done. If not, just summon your courage and approach her if, for nothing else, *just so you'll know.* You want to get it done so you can get the ball rolling and get onto the good stuff. Keep in mind that the sooner you approach her and see if she's interested in you, the sooner you can get on with it.

That's pretty much it. And, I shouldn't have to tell you to never use a pick-up line on a chick, right? Well, don't. Pick-up lines should be laughed at, not used in the hopes of actually picking up a chick. Kinda ironic, isn't it?

And, as always, it's good to act like a gentleman whenever you are in the company of chicks. Just be nice and never insult them. Also, never touch her unless she touches you first and don't misinterpret a slight brush of her arm for a touch. Keep your hands to yourself and always be respectful. When she sees that you pose no immediate threat, she'll relax and let you in a little. And, from there, all you have to do to keep her interested is to talk a little and allow her to talk about herself. So be sure to ask where she's from and how long she's lived there, etc.

The thing is, once you get over your initial shyness, all this will come like second nature. Once you see she isn't going to tear you a new one, you can relax and be happy that you had the nerve to approach her and talk to her.

And then all you have to do is start talking. The conversation might be a little awkward at first, but it always is whenever you first meet someone. Just take it easy and let it flow, asking her questions and listening to her responses and telling her a little about yourself as you go along. After a little bit of this, ask yourself, *Do I want to get to know this girl better?* Do you want to ask her for a date? If so, all you do is ask, "Hey, can I have your number so I can give you a call sometime?" If yes, ask her when is a good time.

And now she will either give it to you or not. If she doesn't give it to you, don't fret, simply excuse yourself and move on. If she does, either write it down or put it in your cell phone and then thank her and say, "Talk to your soon," as you walk away.

Another angle to consider is that she might not be interested in you, even if she's responding to your approach. How do you tell?

How to tell if she's not interested:
- She keeps looking away or over your shoulder.
- She gives you very short answers.
- She declines your offer for a drink.

- She rolls her eyes often.
- She leaves only a few minutes into the conversation.

If you find the girl you've been talking to do any of these things, excuse yourself and let her be. She's not interested but at least you gave it a shot and now you can mark her off the list of potentials. Don't take it personally. You will find that a lot of girls act like this, so don't get discouraged or vow to never talk to another girl again. If you just shrug this off as a part of dating, you will find it gets easier to talk to girls over time. When this happens, life and dating becomes a lot easier and a lot more fun. You're just out to meet people to begin with, right? Keeping an attitude like this will put you ahead of the game.

Now, after you're done approaching a chick or two, pat yourself on the back. It wasn't so hard, was it? And the next time you talk to a chick it will be that much easier.

Making the call after you get the number.

So, you've got the number of some hot chick and now you don't know what to do. You know it's time to make the call. You have her number in hand and wonder how you'll get the nerve to go through with it. You're more nervous now than you were when you approached her. You want to call but you feel like a weirdo and just plain panicky. You're afraid she'll reject you, or, worse, won't remember who you are.

Relax! You are not supposed to be taking all this so seriously! So what if she doesn't remember you? She's probably a hot chick and has lots of guys call her. Just tell her where and when you met, that's all. You don't have to get embarrassed or take offense to this. It's no big deal, after all. You're not marrying this chick, just calling to see if she'd *like* to meet.

Now before you meet, you need to know exactly what you want to do with this chick. Do you want to take her out for a nice meal or just have drinks or coffee somewhere? You need a game plan here so you're not stumbling over your words. If you have a definite plan of what you want to do, then this will give you more confidence to call. Write it down if you have to. Do anything to keep you from forgetting what you're going to say.

So, are you calm now? Good. Pick up the phone, dial her number and wait in agony until she answers. When she answers, say, "Hello, this is _____, and we met at _____. Remember?" Now wait and listen to her response. If she doesn't remember, she might have been drunk or otherwise distracted. No big deal, just overlook this and ask her if she'd like to meet sometime. If you get easily offended at this, keep in mind that you will need to develop a thick skin and learn to not wear your feelings on your sleeve. Besides, do you want these girls to know that they get to you that much? No, you don't.

Now figure out where you want to meet her.

Places you can meet:
- For a cup of coffee.
- For a drink.
- For dinner.
- At the movies.
- At the park.
- At a concert or to see a local band.

Then say, "I was wondering if you'd like to go out sometime?"

And she will either say "yes" or "I'm busy" which is a euphemism for "no thanks." If so, say this, "Well, if you change your mind, you can give me a call. My number is _____." And then tell her you'll talk to her later.

Now if she wants to go, tell her, "Great! Do you want to meet me there or would you like me to pick you up?" Keep in mind that on many first dates, chicks might feel more comfortable meeting you somewhere instead of you picking them up. Give her this option and then if she wants to meet you there, tell her you'll see her then. If she wants you to pick her up, then get her address.

That's pretty much the gist of it.

It's hard, I know, to make that initial call but keep in mind that it only hurts for a little while and then it's all over. Once again, practice makes perfect and the only way you'll ever get good at this is to pick up the phone and do it.

Is she in control?

A big part of dating that us guys overlook is the fact that while we are in charge of asking for the date and arranging it, women are actually the ones in control. This is a big part of dating that a lot of guys don't think about and, thusly, trip themselves up over.

The best thing to do is to realize that women are in control of the date. Once you concede on this, you can relax and enjoy yourself more. This doesn't mean she's going to walk all over you or make fun of you. It just means she's got a lot of the control as far as dating goes. Think about it. She gets to say "yes" to the date—unless she asks you out, of course, which means that she's even more in control. But, besides that, she also gets to say "yes" or "no" to sex or a second date. If that's not control, what is?

How did this happen? Why is the chick in control?

Hate to break it to you, but this has been going on for a while now. Well, it's pretty much been going on since men began to "court" women. Women are usually in control of any relationship from the get-go. She can always say "stop" or "no" and that's exactly what happens. But then again, you can always say stop or go, too. The only difference is that you usually don't want to. For whatever reason, she might and that's why she's in control.

It's a tough row to hoe but absolutely necessary to understand if you are going to date. Of course, it's up to you to ask her out and to, more or less, plan the date, but ultimately it's up to her to go through with it which subsequently determines if it even takes place.

So, allow her to be in control. If she wants to leave the date early, don't argue. If she wants to go to a different restaurant than one you planned, say "okay". However, don't be her whipping boy. The biggest thing is to keep her happy and if this means going along with her whims, then go along as long as they're not taxing you. However, if she's too in control and won't even let you order what you want in a restaurant, then you can start calling the shots and you can do that by telling her you want to end the date early. Or if she starts trying to control the situation in a belittling way— like trying to get you to wear make-up or something—walk away from this one. Some girls do stuff like this to humiliate guys and I, personally, wouldn't want any part of this. Or you could subtly assert yourself a little to begin with. Keep in mind that your date might not be aware of what she's doing. However, if she's acting like a controlling diva, you have the option to end the date. If she's too much of a hassle, then she's probably going to be more work than she's worth. You can finish your date but with someone like this, I wouldn't call her back for a second one.

But don't get scared because most women are not going to be this bad. Most will like it when you take charge with the dinner plans. This shows her that you've been thinking about your date and planning for it and that you want to please her. Hey, keep doing that and she'll want to stick around and please you, too.

How to act on the date.

Let's say you've got the date and now you don't know what to do. You're uncertain about yourself and afraid you'll somehow offend her. To that I say, "Relax!" If you make a flub and do something that makes you look like an ass, join the club. We've all done that. It's how you recover that's key to how the date ends up. If you apologize and just shrug it off, all the better. This lets her know that you can handle the ups and downs of meeting someone new.

If you find that you're very nervous before the date even begins, take a moment to yourself and inhale a few calming breaths before your date and get yourself mentally prepared for it. Don't go in thinking this chick needs to be that impressed with you or you'll liable to psyche yourself out. Just relax. Sure, try to give off a good impression, but don't get so worked up about doing it that you dissolve into a mass of nerves.

However, there are a few simple things you can do so you'll know the date will go smoothly, and they are…

- Always give her a nice smile as soon as she opens the door or meets you in the restaurant.
- Always tell her she looks "nice" or "lovely" or whatever adjective you feel fits at the time.

- Always bring her a small bouquet of flowers or a nice, small box of good chocolates.
- Always dress nicely and be sure to shower, shave and groom beforehand.
- Always check your manners and be sure that you're on your best behavior.
- Always open her door and hold the door open for her, letting her enter first.

There are other little things you can do and I'm sure you've got a list of your own. If not, take from mine or make your own. The main thing to do is to be polite and act gentlemanly. Also, keep in mind that there are some things that are universally bad to do on a date. And they are below...

Some things you should never do:
- Chew gum.
- Smoke. However, keep in mind that she might smoke and if so, it shouldn't be a big deal to smoke in front of her. If so, let her make the first move in t his direction.
- Curse.
- Pass gas.
- Ask rude, personal questions about sex or her private life.
- Ask for sex or even a kiss on the first date.

It's mostly about using common sense. If you think you're doing something "wrong", then don't do it. It's that simple. If you think you've said something insulting, just apologize for it. And don't get hung up on it either. Just let it go and write it off to first date jitters.

The main thing to focus on is staying calm and taking a few deep breaths throughout the evening whenever you feel a little nervous. Remember, as the evening progresses, your nervousness will subside and then you'll begin to enjoy the company of your date. And that's really the whole point of going out in the first place, isn't it?

Now let's say the date went well, but now that it's over, what do you do? As you're parting ways, ascertain if you like this chick enough to go on a second date. If not, don't tell her you'll call her as that's just really lame. And, no, you don't have to have an excuse. Simply say, "Good night."

If you do want to see her again, then tell her so. You can say something like, "By the way, I had a great time and would love to do this if again if you're up for it." More than likely, she'll want another date. If so, she'll nod and say "Sure." And then all you have to do is say, "Then I'll call you later to set it up."

Now that's over, what about a good night kiss? I wouldn't go for it this early in the game as it seems a little too forward to some chicks and you can never tell which ones will take offense. If she wants to kiss you, she will let you know by tilting her head up to yours. If she doesn't do that, back off. I wouldn't even try to kiss her on the cheek if she's giving the vibe off that she's uncomfortable in any way. It's odd, but some girls will be put off by even a kiss on the cheek. Not all, mind you, but some. It's best just to play it by ear in these cases.

So, the date's over and it's time to go home. You've had a good night and should be proud of yourself. You went through with it! You didn't throw up with nerves! You held the door open for her and you paid for dinner. She smiled a lot and wants a second date.

It feels good, doesn't it? Congratulations and welcome to the wonderful world of dating chicks. It's fun, isn't it? The great thing about dating is that it does make you feel like a man and it makes you feel like you've accomplished something. And, just think, all you had to do was make that initial move off the couch and into your new life. With that first step comes great things, right? Right. Now just don't get too over-confident or chicken out the next time and you will do just fine.

The first kiss.

Now that the date's over and you've gone through all that preliminary stuff, it might just be time for your first kiss. The best advice I can tell you on this is to take the lead and give her a kiss worth coming back for more.

You will know when it's time for your first kiss, usually after the second date. (Of course, as all women are different, keep in mind that she might want to wait until the third or forth date, which may seem strange, though it does happen.) So, after the date is done and you're getting ready to part ways, summon your courage and go in for the kiss. She should be ready for this and shouldn't turn away. If her face is turned towards yours, she probably wants the kiss. If so, proceed. And have fun with it!

The most important thing to do is to just go with the flow. Be aware of her body language. If she's moving in closer and closer to you as your date progresses, she probably wants to be kissed, and soon. However, do not start groping after the first kiss. Wait and see what she does first. And, if she's the one who gropes? Lucky you. Have fun.

Don't try to rush her into sex.

So, what about sex? Look, most chicks don't like to kiss on the first date, so it's highly unlikely they'll jump in the sack with you this early. I wouldn't even consider this an option until the third or fourth or even later date. Just put it out of your mind for now. This is the best way to go so you don't look too over-eager or come off as bit of a pervert. So, just sit back and let the date unfold and allow it to go in whichever direction it might. More than likely, it's not going to end up in the bedroom.

Sorry, I know that hurts but take it from me, this is one hard truth about dating. This isn't to say it won't happen; it's just more than likely it won't.

It's also a bit immature to think that you might have sex with someone you've only dated once. That stuff rarely happens in real life, though it seems to happen a lot in the movies. But, of course, you should never confuse the world of cinema with real life. That stuff is just for plot and to keep the audience interested. In real life, most guys have to wait a few times before having sex.

Sooner or later, she'll probably want to have sex. And, yes, she'll probably make you wait a while for it, if she gives it to you at all. But, hey, that's the roll of the dice. You take your chances and see what comes up. Same thing with dating. You could go out with ten or twenty or more chicks before one gives it up.

Do you know one reason a chick might make you wait for sex is because she likes you a lot and wants to keep you hanging on? This isn't true in every case, but it does happen. So, if she isn't giving it up so easily, it might be because she likes you, really, really likes you.

On the other hand, there will be some girls who will have sex on the first date. This is rare and if it happens to you, don't read anything into it unless she definitely wants to go out again. Also, don't judge her and never call again if you get this lucky. It doesn't mean she's a slut or anything, it just means she really likes you and doesn't want to wait. She might just be a really sexually active girl. Regardless, it's up to you to take advantage of the situation or not.

How to tell if a chick is interested in you.

We discussed this briefly in a previous chapter, but I wanted to go a little more in depth. How do you know if a chick is interested in you? Some chicks are hard to gauge and you'll never know whether or not they like you until you, of course, stop showing interest in them and then they'll ask, "Why haven't you called?" It's a Catch-22 but one a guy must endure.

Besides that, it's sort of hard to tell if a woman is interested in you. I know some guys think just because a girl is nice and tells them the time of day she's interested, which is not usually the case. I also know that women can be nice and flirty and not think anything about it and then wonder why you thought they liked you.

Chicks are hard to figure out and, on this subject, you more or less have to go on a gut feeling. Unless, of course, she comes right out and tells you she likes you. It can sometimes be hard to tell as it's almost an instinctual thing. But there are times when you know when a girl likes you the same way you know if you like a girl—she shows you interest.

In the end, it's that easy. If she likes you, she will show you interest. She'll ask you questions and be a little chatty and flirty. There are other ways to tell, too, of course.

A list to gauge if she's interested or not:
- She will flirt with you.
- She will smile at you for no reason.
- She will lift her eyebrows and stare at you from the corner of her eye.
- She will "accidentally" brush up against you.
- She will find ways to start a conversation.
- She will play with or toss her hair.
- She will ask you about you and what your plans are for the weekend.
- She doesn't ever try to avoid you in any way.

It's pretty straightforward. Women, as I've said, aren't that much different from guys. If you can wrap your head around this, dating will be so much easier. Look at her as a person, not as someone you want to conquer. Look at her as a potential friend and not just as a lover. If she likes you, she's looking at you the same way.

What if she's not interested?

It happens. You went on a date, which you thought was good. You had a nice time and you thought she liked you. But now, it seems, she's avoiding you and not returning your calls. What's a guy to do?

Stop calling her. That's it. Just stop calling her. Don't "accidentally" drop by places you think she might be. Forget about her. Move on. If you don't, you are headed for major trouble.

If you start "dropping by" a chick's house a few times a week or calling her house a couple dozen times a day, you are stalking her. This leads to trouble. Sometimes, we guys become obsessed with a chick simply based on the fact that we don't understand why she doesn't like us. Don't torture yourself. Believe me, it isn't worth it. If she doesn't like you, forget about her.

I can't emphasize this enough. I've seen a few guys go down this road only to be yelled at by some chick and called a stalker. The thing is, the more you stalk, the more creeped out she gets. If she feels too threatened, she will call the police.

I don't know why some guys become obsessed with some chicks. It's odd to me, but it does seem to happen sometimes. Maybe they think she's the only woman in the world or something, but she isn't.

If you find yourself doing this, do something else. Talk it out with a buddy or go hiking. Do something to get her out of your mind. The best thing to do is go out and try to find another one. When you see that this chick doesn't make or break you, your obsession will go away. It's really that simple.

On the other side of this, there might be a chick that can't get *you* out of her mind. She might just turn into psycho-stalker-chick. If you have this happen to you—and it does happen—I feel for you. What can you do in this situation? You have to put her straight and tell her you're not interested. The best thing would be to, of course, avoid this situation altogether. However, it's only after you meet that you realize you've got a stalker on your hands.

So, just keep your radar up for any erratic behavior at first. If you go out with a chick and she flips out a lot or seems psycho, go with your gut and then leave the date early, claiming a stomach bug or whatever you have to do. The sooner you can get out of her field of vision, the better off you will be.

Also, it's good to keep in mind that not every girl you run across is going to be interested in you. We all know this, but I know some guys do get a little desperate. These guys tend to think that just because a girl smiles at them or does something like glance their way that they want to date them. No, no and no. if a girl is being nice, just take it for that—she's just being nice. Until you know she really has a genuine interest in you, don't assume anything, especially if you haven't even talked yet. If you're a little too desperate to date, you can misconstrue a woman's actions. So, the best thing to do is hold back and then, after you approach and talk to her, ascertain if she likes you or not.

The bottom line is this: It's always a good thing to listen to your gut instinct. Even if you find you're the one obsessed, your gut is probably telling you to stop. So, listen to it and follow it. Usually, it won't let you go wrong. Also, listen to your gut if you start feeling a little desperate and never just assume any girl likes you just because she gave you the time of day. It's best to wait these things out a little and not make any assumptions.

Wanna come over?

A guy's place can be his sanctuary. It's where we sleep, eat and watch TV. Usually, we don't really care how it looks or smells. However, when you start dating, it's more than likely that women will want to come over. When this happens, you need to be sure your place is in good shape and ready for visitors.

Two situations.

The first situation: After a date, you want to still talk to this chick, even if doesn't mean sex but it's getting late and everything is closing. Well, you can either take her to an all-night coffee shop or you can invite her back to your place.

The second situation: Say, you've been seeing a chick for a few dates and would like to invite her over to your place for a date but don't know exactly what to do with her once you get her there. You're thinking about cooking her dinner, but don't know exactly what that entails.

Well, the first thing to ascertain is if you'd be comfortable with her seeing where you live. Take a look around your place. Does it look like a bomb just went off? If so, clean it up. Throw out any clutter and be sure to dust and vacuum everything. Another big thing to do is clean the bathroom like you were in the military. Chicks detest disgusting bathrooms. This also means cleaning the tub because they are sure to look behind the shower curtain.

And clean out the medicine cabinet, too, especially if you have some things in there like anti-fungal crème you might not want her to know about. Believe me, she will probably look. Curiosity gets the best of us. And women are extremely curious about everything.

One major thing to have in the bathroom is toilet paper and some hand soap and a clean hand towel on the sink so she can wash and dry her hands.

You don't have to spring clean or anything like that, just make sure you place clean and presentable. If you have a dog or cat, vacuum up any hairs off the sofa and clean the litter box.

Another good thing to have on hand is a bottle of wine and some cheese and crackers to snack on or some other finger food like that. If she doesn't drink, buy some sodas or bottled water to offer her. Or you can buy some good coffee and make her a cup of joe. Having some creamer and sugar on hand is also a good idea if she's a coffee drinker.

Since you probably won't want to watch TV, unless she's coming over to watch a movie or something, have some good chick music to listen to. I wouldn't recommend Barry White right off because that's just a little too obvious. However, do out put on something smooth and light. Just don't go too hard-core or punk rock on her, unless she's that kind of girl and into that kind of music.

Now I'm not promising anything, but it might be a good idea to buy a new box of condoms just in case. You never know when a man and woman get together what's going to happen and you want to be prepared. Having sex can make babies and if you don't want a baby just yet, get some spermicidal condoms. Also, it's a good idea to keep these stashed somewhere pretty well hidden because you don't want her seeing them and getting the wrong idea, like you think she's a slut or you're a sex fiend.

Even if you *don't* think that things might progress in this way, always wash your sheets and blankets beforehand. You never know when you might get lucky and you definitely don't want to turn her off with unclean bed linens. Dirty linens can be a real mood killer, if you know what I mean. So, just wash these things and make your bed look clean and comfortable.

If you're inviting her over for dinner and have no clue as how to cook anything that isn't microwave friendly, why not ask mom? Mom usually knows simple, good things to cook. If not, why not just have her favorite food delivered?

Once you've eaten, have a few classic movies on hand to watch, if you like. Or, perhaps, a board game. The point is that you're spending quality time with her and that doesn't mean your activities have to be over-thought or over-wrought. It just means that whatever you do, you'll probably have a good time because at this stage, you more than likely like each other pretty well.

While you're not trying sweep her off her feet by doing all this, you are showing her you aren't a slob who lives like a bum. You're showing her that you can pick up after yourself and can have a few food items on hand in case she gets hungry. You're simply being a good host. This will surely impress her and she might want to spend more time at your place if she feels comfortable there.

Sex.

Sex is something all guys are looking for from the moment we lay eyes on a chick. Did you know this is what she's thinking too? Sure, she might be thinking marriage and babies, but you can't have babies without sex. So, keep in mind that she's thinking about sex, even if it's not in the exact same way you are and even if it's more on a subconscious level.

Sex can be a very nerve-wrecking business. However, the best thing about sex is that as you're doing it, you're not really thinking about doing it. You're just doing it. All the nervousness resides in the build-up *before* sex.

The best advice I can give you is to do your best. It doesn't hurt to study techniques in porn movies, but those movies aren't really that close to reality. You're a guy and probably have been laid before. If you haven't, then watch erotic movies or read books specifically written about sex for guys and how to do it. The thing about sex is that unless you've done it, it's hard to tell someone how to do it. It's a very natural, instinctual thing.

Taking charge in the bedroom is a guy's job. You have to be willing to initiate that first kiss. She will follow if she wants it, too. After the first kiss goes well, you're both probably expecting sex at some time in the near future. This can be daunting. But like I've said with everything else, relax! This is supposed to be fun, not something that's going to give you an ulcer.

Sex is one of the best things in a relationship, for both partners. But in order to have good sex, and have her want more where that came from, you do have to work at it a little. This means taking care of her needs first. The biggest thing to do is get a chick ready for sex. This means foreplay. She needs foreplay to get ready for sex. She needs it in order to allow you to have sex with her. If you take your time and get her ready, she will let you take your time to get your rocks off.

When you first initiate sex with a woman, take time to kiss her slowly and sensually. Let her know you're not going anywhere until she's pleased. Be sure to pay attention to the neck area, kissing and sucking on it. This really gets to most chicks and helps them to overcome some of their initial shyness.

Another area to concentrate on is the sides of her face. Run the sides of your hands down her face as you kiss her, then take them on down to other parts of her body.

I won't give you a play by play because most guys aren't going to memorize something like this anyway. And they won't because sex comes naturally once it gets started. There's not much explaining to do because sex is pretty much self-explanatory.

The gist is to please her first. Mostly, it's about paying attention to her needs before you pay attention to yours. Get her going and she'll let you keep going.

If you find yourself a little, shall we say, "quick on the draw", consider masturbating beforehand. This might help you relax more and maybe not be too eager and geared up if something actually happens. Being prepared in this way can make the evening more fun and exciting and, invariably, make it last a little longer.

Sex should be fun and exciting and it usually is. If you sense at any time she's really not into it, don't force it. Move back and allow her to change her mind. Then she might come to you. Keep in mind that her nerves might be eating at her and not allowing her to relax enough to enjoy what's happening. But showing her that you can wait and you don't have to "have it" makes her feel more secure with you. This builds trust and as soon as she's ready, she'll let you have it.

So, be a gentleman and see what happens. Sex is a great thing, especially when it's shared between two people who really like—or love—one another. Not pushing it on her and being willing to wait shows most chicks that you're a stand-up guy. Sex is important but not important enough to ruin a potential good relationship over.

This goes without saying, but if you have sex, be sure to use protection. Condoms, particularity. You can get many diseases from having unprotected sex. Use your best subject and always use a condom.

In the end, take sex as it comes and never force sex. I know guys want it all the time but sometimes, waiting is the best part. It really is because, once you do get to have sex with a chick you really like, it's like a million fireworks going off at once. Believe me, I know this to be true.

Is she the one? Love.

How do you know if you love a chick? That's easy. You want to marry her and, possibly, have babies with her. If you love her, you can't get her out of your mind and you want to make sure she's okay all the time. You wonder what she's doing and what she's thinking about when she's not with you. You want to buy her stuff and show her all the things you're good at. You want to spend a lot of time with her. You want to buy her an engagement ring. You get jealous when other guys look at her "like that".

Have you experienced anything like that? If so, she's got your heart, buddy, and there's not much you can do about it.

So, how about those words, "I love you"? What about them? Do you want to say them? If so, say them. Of course, you shouldn't say them after your first date, but you'll know when the time is right. Also, you'll know if she'd digging you, too.

The thing about love is that it can really make you feel like a good person. It can make you happy. Love is great, just like everyone says. So, if you love her, not only say it but show it. That means going out for her favorite donuts or coffee in the early morning hours. That means buying her "special" little gifts occasionally and letting her use the shower first so there's plenty of hot water. Believe me, little things like this will be very much appreciated.

On the other hand, this doesn't mean being her lapdog. If she starts to try to control you, back off and tell her you won't put up with that nonsense. Women are usually controlling because they're naturally bossy but that doesn't give her a license to make your life miserable. If you find her becoming overbearing, sit down and have a talk with her about it. Tell her how you feel and don't worry about her stomping out. If she storms out and she really loves you, she'll walk back in a few hours. If she doesn't come back? Then she wasn't meant for you. Sorry.

Whatever you do, take this time early in your relationship to really let it grow. Don't rush anything. Don't push her into marriage or moving in together. Don't let her push you, either. However, if you're ready for something like this, then do it. Why wait if you feel it's right? When it's right, you know it and I don't see any reason to postpone it at all.

The thing about a good relationship is that neither of you have to play games nor wait on the other to get the same idea you have. Take love as it comes, just as you have life and great things will unfold on their own.

Some things women do.

Women love to talk. From time to time, she will want to have little discussions about this or that. It might be the fact that you leave socks on the floor or were late picking her up or whatever. Don't get upset when this happens. Just expect her to want these heart to heart discussions. Women love to communicate and if they don't think you two are communicating "well", she'll do her best to remedy that.

So, yes, she will want to have a "talk" sometime. She will want to know your plans for the future and if they include her. She will sometimes drive you up the wall and sometimes she will push you to the brink of insanity. She will test you just to watch you fail. And why does she do all this? Because this is a woman's job—to drive men crazy.

Whatever she does, just don't let it get under your skin, though that is easier said than done. Love isn't an easy thing sometimes and that means putting up with stuff that drives you batty. The best thing to do is keep your cool, back off and tell her she's pushing your buttons. If she keeps making you crazy, the best thing to do is get away from her for a few hours. Tell her you're going to let her cool down and when you come back, she should be fine.

Keep in mind that you need to be aware that women are different from guys. They aren't necessarily so even-keeled and stable all the time. Sometimes, they do have their little breakdowns and cry and throw tantrums. Many of them will go crazy from time to time for no real reason or for things so insignificant that they make no sense. Don't take this to heart when it happens! This is just your woman being a woman. Sometimes she will act like she hates your guts and sometimes she'll burn your toast on purpose. Again, it's just a woman being a woman. Don't try to rationalize it! Just let it go and walk away until she's herself again.

We could say all this is due to hormones and PMS or whatever. But I don't try to rationalize it. I don't believe it's our job to understand why until they tell us.

Women will mystify you, just as they do most other guys. One minute she's lovable and the next, not so much. Some days she will make you laugh and other days she will make you hate life. Some days you will love her more than anything and other days, you will wonder what you saw in her. But when she smiles at you, you'll get why you love her all over again. And probably find more reasons to love her.

The most important thing to do if and when she goes nuts from time to time is to listen to her. Just sit and listen and offer your input whenever necessary. By doing this, she will know you are hearing her, which is one for the most important things a guy can do for his girl. When she's had her say, tell her in a calm voice what you think. Try not to be accusatory. Try to be gentle and loving, though it might be hard. Don't blow your top. Just get through this. Soon, it will be over and things will be back to normal.

So why all the drama? It's just life, so welcome to it. This is called being in a relationship. There is good and there is bad. Take it as it comes, even if it's making you crazy right now and know that it will soon pass and you can get back to the good stuff soon.

Do you want to get married?

One of the first things we discussed in this book was your motivations for dating. One of the main ones for many guys is marriage. Sure, they want to date around a little before settling down, but for some, it's their main motivation.

If marriage is what you're looking for, you have to find a girl who wants the same thing. Once you do that—and you'll know when—you can tie the knot and start a life together.

When you've found "the one" you want to marry, you'll know it. And if you want to ask her to marry you, do it. She might be waiting on you to do just and most of the time, because you're in a serious relationships, she will not be too surprised. Though she will be very happy.

Marriage seems scary to most guys, but really, it isn't. Being with the same person for the rest of your life may seem like an eternity, but if you're with the right girl, it won't seem like any time at all. If this is something you really want, go for it once you're ready.

However, don't let her pressure you into it. Some chicks will try to do this. If you're not ready to get married, be upfront and honest about it. Don't lead her on. Just tell her. Be warned that she might break up with you. If so, that's the breaks. It is the consequence you have to suffer.

But, as I've said, if you're not ready, let her go so she can find a guy who *is* ready. Don't waste your time or hers. It's not fair to either one of you if you're stringing her along.

If you do want to ask her to marry you, do it in a special way. I'm sure there are a thousand things you can do like take her to a park for a picnic or relive your first date. Of course, you will want to have an engagement ring on hand. You might not be able to afford a big one. However, if she's in love with you, it won't matter as long as *you're* the one giving her the ring. You can give it to her with the promise of a better one some day. Just be sure to come through with that promise later on, though.

In the end, it's up to you to do the asking. Just figure out if you want to or not and then proceed in the way that best suits you.

Chicks understood.

I think that about covers it. While this isn't an encyclopedia of chicks, it does cover most everything you need to know about how to understand them. But the most important lesson to learn is that you have to get out there and do it, if you ever want a relationship or want to date. It is up to you to get the ball rolling and up to you to ask for that first date. Without ever taking the initiative, how can you ever know what will be?

Chicks are work, you have to understand that. Dating is work but it's also a labor of love. You have to be willing to put in the work in order to get the rewards. You have to have a big interest in doing it before you can start. You can make it into a hobby, if you like, or as a way of getting to know women better. The point is to get out there and get it done. No one will do it for you.

So, get out there and get to it. The chicks are waiting.

Printed in the United Kingdom
by Lightning Source UK Ltd.
128586UK00001B/152/A